MW00777387

Creating an Undergraduate Literary Journal

Creating an Undergraduate Literary Journal

A Production Guide for Students and Faculty

Audrey Colombe

BLOOMSBURY ACADEMIC
LONDON • NEW YORK • OXFORD • NEW DELHI • SYDNEY

BLOOMSBURY ACADEMIC
Bloomsbury Publishing Plc
50 Bedford Square, London, WC1B 3DP, UK
1385 Broadway, New York, NY 10018, USA
29 Earlsfort Terrace, Dublin 2, Ireland

BLOOMSBURY, BLOOMSBURY ACADEMIC and the Diana logo are
trademarks of Bloomsbury Publishing Plc

First published in Great Britain 2022

Copyright © Audrey Colombe, 2022

Audrey Colombe has asserted her right under the Copyright,
Designs and Patents Act, 1988, to be identified as Author of this work.

For legal purposes the Acknowledgments on p. viii constitute
an extension of this copyright page.

Cover design: Eleanor Rose
Student magazine covers supplied by the author | Background
photograph by Laura Chouette on Unsplash

All rights reserved. No part of this publication may be reproduced or
transmitted in any form or by any means, electronic or mechanical, including
photocopying, recording, or any information storage or retrieval system,
without prior permission in writing from the publishers.

Bloomsbury Publishing Plc does not have any control over, or responsibility for,
any third-party websites referred to or in this book. All internet addresses given
in this book were correct at the time of going to press. The author and publisher
regret any inconvenience caused if addresses have changed or sites have ceased
to exist, but can accept no responsibility for any such changes.

A catalogue record for this book is available from the British Library.

A catalog record for this book is available from the Library of Congress.

ISBN: HB: 978-1-3501-6069-9
         PB: 978-1-3501-6070-5
       ePDF: 978-1-3501-6071-2
      eBook: 978-1-3501-6072-9

Typeset by Integra Software Services Pvt. Ltd.
Printed and bound in Great Britain

To find out more about our authors and books visit www.bloomsbury.com
and sign up for our newsletters.

For student editors and their advisors

CONTENTS

ACKNOWLEDGMENTS

The idea for this book first came from David Avital. Lucy Brown saw it through. Every colleague and student mentioned in this book, thank you. Derrick Austin, Kim Coy, Shaina Frazier, Grace Wagner, LeeAnne Carlsen, Kay Cosgrove, Cait Weiss Orcutt, Matthew Salesses, and so many others— it's been a joy to recall the work.

Introduction

This guide is written to assist undergraduate editors and their advisors and/or instructors. It is also for writers who want to understand periodical publication processes and do a little editing themselves. It is the result of many years spent as a faculty advisor for undergraduate literary magazines, at many institutions of higher learning in several different US states and at many types of colleges and universities (private, public, large and small). I have busily watched student editors do their magic—watched them engage the work with amazing energy. I have also instructed, prompted, cajoled, praised, and challenged hundreds of staff members—and learned from them. For me, and I hope for the reader, this book is the result of a fruitful, collective, nomadic journey.

Undergraduate editors I have worked with have moved through their literary editorships rather quickly while I've moved institutions at a slightly slower pace. As I've experienced them, student editors who showed up to do the work are fantastic (and complicated) wonderful word-nerds who share distinct similarities. For starters, they are noticeably driven by a love of language and a sense of obligation to fellow writers. In literary circles the latter has been called literary citizenship—more on that later. The new writer-publishers want to respond in "print" to the moment, to what their cohort has to say and wants to do within publishing. It has less to do with the big publishing companies and more to do with local and direct need. Thank the stars for that. The broader array of intentions that contribute to their literary citizenship may come mostly from a need to understand what publishing is, but also a strong desire to feature the work of new writers like themselves, to build a sense of community they feel strongly about engaging, plus a desire to understand what happens to their own work in the process of getting started with publication. The work, in other words, is theirs. I am simply institutional staff (with tenure, which helps when we wander to stickier political areas) reporting here on what I have seen—such as very lengthy and heated arguments, sometimes in my living room, on the Oxford comma. Hardly interested in calling a winner in those competitions, I have nearly fainted with the realization of my good fortune: how many professors get to witness, on a regular basis, their undergraduates discussing grammar and mechanics with the raucous pleasure usually reserved for divas on a runway?

On their vision, however, I run to keep up—offering academic support in the form of articles they can read to support their view of *keeping the door open for disparate writers,* of connections in the community for new initiatives for writers from across the spectrum, of networks they can build in and out of academia to support exciting new voices—and then cheer them on as they push forward. Several former editors will certainly raise an eyebrow at my claim of merely following, of keeping observer status. I believe I have been accused more than once of being too close, too involved, too opinionated on certain matters. Many faculty advisors keep a cooler distance than I do, yes. And of course it is false to claim that the students' interests are always the same as mine in this enterprise. I may digress on that subject elsewhere in this text (Chapter 3). The dedication of this book, however, should make it exceedingly clear: I am in awe of (and humbled by) the students who have shown up, time and time again, to do the work of editing and producing a collection of creative work *of their choosing.* This is their project, first and foremost, enacted inside an institution of higher education—with all the complications thereof.

Caught up in my meddling, I have tried to sit back and learn things, big things about people in general and smaller things about individuals. No matter how fully functional the editors have been, or how often they have pulled disappearing acts (I can only recall that happening twice, years apart and long ago), they were all devoted, forcefully and actively interested in the work that I hope I helped them do. They brought their skills and found new ones, every time. Many of the Editors-in-Chief I have worked with, to my knowledge, continued professionally in the area of literacy, literary arts, and/or wordsmithing. How lucky I am to have spent time with them. This book is my homage to them.

On the subject of time passing and what everyone is now doing, day to day, this guide will be useful only as it is a record of what had been going on with undergraduate literary magazines up to the time of the Covid-19 pandemic and the growth of the Black Lives Matter (BLM) movement, which arrived at about the same time as this text was being completed. A bit of what has happened to the literary arts as it surrounds and shifts through the pandemic, plus the opportunities gained by the Black Lives Matter movement, has been included here during revisions. What happens next with publishing, education, and the culture of what we call the literary arts here in the United States is anyone's guess, but everyone I have discussed it with believes that while changes in the structures of the literary establishment may be significant, nothing much is likely to change in people's reading habits and their curiosity about trying out their own dreams on the page or screen. Although we may get more interesting material to read as publishing reshapes itself to answer the call for more kinds of texts and wider subject matter, the pandemic and the Black Lives Matter movement have required of us a revision of our everyday—the pandemic pulling us away from each other and BLM pushing us toward one other. Thank goodness, and not a moment too early in the realm of realizing the wealth that has always been there (the array of writers and their skills) and the fragility of what we loosely call humanity. There is no doubt in my mind that future incarnations of student literary endeavors will include a new set of creative solutions as they get busy reinvigorating the literary landscape. Ten years from now undergraduate literary magazines might look very different. I hope this book may still be useful in that future, however, as it describes the connecting parts of an organization that recognizes itself as mutable, serious, and driven by creativity.

A couple of notes on the text: I use the phrase "university or college" frequently. I mean that some institutions call themselves "university" while others call themselves "college"—as in Sarah Lawrence College. When I write "university or college" I tend to alternate with "institution" because there are places like MIT (Massachusetts Institute of Technology) or FIT (Florida Institute of Technology) who are also members of the higher ed realm. However (let me back down the ladder a rung or two), when I use the word "college" alone, I am referring to the section of the university that houses a collection of departments and is led by a dean, also known as an "academic unit" (one of several, usually with "college" in the title somewhere) that is collected under the auspices of a chief academic officer or provost. While larger universities tend to have several colleges, they don't always work with each other closely, though most universities are asked on a regular basis to please do more of that—so I hope I have covered the circumstance here. When I use the term "upper editor" I mean the collection of section editors (fiction, reviews, poetry, nonfiction, web, etc.), the leaders of separate editing groups, along with the managing editor(s) and Editor-in-Chief, which I capitalize because the person who takes on that job has my undying respect and can stand a bit of formal recognition.

I occasionally refer to a "graduate advisor," which is another way of saying that a university has seen fit to assign a teaching assistant (TA) to the undergraduate literary magazine enterprise. This kind of TA assignment is underutilized. If your department has graduate students with teaching assistantships—even in literature, art, communication, or composition and rhetoric (in other words, if you have no creative writing graduate students)—I encourage you to look into arranging a literary magazine assistantship assignment for your TAs, perhaps in some combination with the usual teaching assignment (first-year writing being the standard in English departments) that graduate students are famous for. This kind of TA-ship is a marvelous idea for graduate students (teaching by hands-on example and including arts administration experience) and very helpful to the undergraduates (who get to know the graduate students in a work environment while taking advantage of their further skills in the literary, media, or visual arts). This kind of assignment signals not only the university's imprimatur on the undergraduate literary arts magazine but a recognition of what the graduate students are there to do: write, create, publish, and work with students and/ or nonprofit organizations like schools, universities, and community arts organizations. As higher ed changes to meet the needs of students who are launching into an uncertain marketplace (and, currently, fewer restaurant jobs), one could effectively argue that experience with content writing, arts, teaching, and copy editing (working with texts and editors online) will serve graduate students quite well. To have undergraduates and graduate students work on their skills together, enacting their different levels of study in a healthy workplace model, hauls new learning structures into this century like nothing else I've seen—because the students bring the ingredients.

To stay with that thread for a moment, universities that recognize the utility of instructing undergraduates in professional realms (i.e., English departments who focus the learning that's being done, and, at least in part, on the work their alums are doing) can turn toward their undergraduate literary magazines as a useful and exciting center of educational development. First, the work students do on a literary magazine comes directly from the classroom study of literature and writing. Undergraduate literary magazines are providing an active context to the material studied: they move student skills toward professionalization—taking with them vital critical and theoretical learning. Plus, putting so much of the work-activity online—publishing it— departments can make available the range of research projects going on in their departments to the general public (an important piece of the digital humanities, if you will). In addition, fore-fronting the technological skills of undergraduates is a very reasonable step in the development of learning strategies in higher ed right now, which pairs well with traditional deep reading and research. (There is a vast and untapped wealth of technological skills the undergraduates show up with, just waiting to exercise—plus the new skills they are learning in just about any academic department moving students through learning and research to applied studies.) A publishing practicum class (many colleges and universities with student publications already run practicum classes) further orients the students to the national conversation about publishing (talk about change! Note the list of books about editing, useful for a publishing practicum course, in Appendix B), adding another layer of professional context to the enterprise of reading and research.

The faculty advisor, then, turns a service activity (advising a student organization or a department publication) into a classroom experience. This is another vital piece of the structure: institutional support via tenured faculty presence. That level of institutional commitment—a faculty member whose workload includes student engagement in professional activities—is necessary. Assuming the advisor teaches the publishing practicum, which is fairly common, an off-load attached to an advising duty is also a good idea when the practicum isn't possible (being released from teaching one course when advising the journal during the production of an issue). Tenured faculty matters because they have institutional knowledge, publishing experience, and serve as a protective barrier when/if students are questioned on their work. Committing a tenured faculty member to the project signals the department's reasonable investment in professional outcomes. A faculty advisor for a student publication is at minimum necessary; a tenured member is true commitment. A graduate student—graduate advisor—helps tremendously but simply doesn't have the institutional knowledge—all by themselves—or the longer-term investment or connections, that a tenured or even tenure-track faculty member has. A faculty advisor who teaches a publication practicum course as a centerpiece of undergraduate curriculum can even function as a curriculum exploder, showing the departments what the project has wrought via their study courses. What better way to find out that your students are learning, which lessons stuck, what the concepts look like in the three-dimensional world of the office workspace and online presence? A student-run literary magazine, woven into curriculum (perhaps all majors have to join the staff for one semester, minimum) could better prepare students for internships as well. I simply don't see a downside for student literary arts publications, especially for English departments holding on to models of study that focus on the artistic merits (and attending theories and criticisms) of the written word over time. "Cultural Studies" is the newer term, though it might reflect the same thing: what are we thinking about (writing about) and valuing right now?

That was certainly a mouthful, but I believe it 100 percent. Rows of desks and twenty-page papers are not going to get our students where they need to go. The world is more chaotic and interesting, and so are the students—and so is a practicum course where students arrive with ideas and produce a publication, even in barely controlled chaos (more on this at the end of Chapter 5).

Preparing the students for a traditional literary publishing job is a related matter, and perhaps as urgent. I know of one former student Editor-in-Chief who recently started her own publishing company. Need I say more: we need these new voices.

As long as we communicate through text there will be a place for people who are fascinated with usage and its variants as well as proofreaders with microscopic vision and a style sheet in hand. For those student editors who are interested in the cultural contribution of long-form texts (novels and biographies and the like—books that have traditionally made money) there will be an industry, still, though it might look a little different. (We hope!) Professional commercial publishing has been going through contortions for several decades now. (Was it ever a static enterprise?) Before the turn of the twenty-first century the large publishing houses converged (crashed, collided, and collapsed) while smaller publishers and the plethora of imprints at commercial houses (plus private boutique publishers and university presses) put out new books at an amazing rate. As readers become recognized as more varied and complex (the recent interest in the voices of marginalized persons has put a spotlight on the very limited vision of big publishers) the market for more fictions and poetries and non-narrative-driven lyric nonfictions might even break down the old distinctions between the "genres." Just ask the students.

Recent convulsions in higher ed, especially the pandemic pitch toward online learning, have not hit undergraduates as hard as they've hit the administration, staff, and faculty—and that's wonderful news. I hope we now get to take the best parts of the reactive situation, together, into new considerations about learning and the work of students—through collective conversation as well as trial and error. As long as the United States can still find an advantage in public ownership of research and development, including in the humanities, higher ed will survive. Student-centered learning has been a popular concept for decades. We know classrooms are no longer distribution centers for information but sites for active learning. Now the workplace has been split into fragments. What a perfect time to communicate at greater reach using the meticulous intent that institutions of higher learning are known for.

1

Defining Your Journal

Whether you are starting a new literary journal or have inherited one that's been in existence for a while, it can be useful to look around at what is available to help you define your project going forward. This means looking back as well as seizing the moment.

All colleges and universities, programs and organizations, have a culture—a collection of people and ideas, landscape and architecture, that give the place a distinct character. For starters, you might take a look at your institution's mission statement: how might your journal move this commitment forward? Your college or university (even departments have mission statements) is probably nonprofit, so who do they serve and why? Who do you want to support, and why? Later, when you are making a pitch for support for your journal, knowing the fit of your project with the institution's mission (or department's, for journals already established) might help you get attention, funding, even recognition.

The community around you—the city, town, and/or state—may also contribute to the identity of the journal. Even the moment in history, the vibe of the times, says something about where you are and what's possible. (What is happening on social media, right now, in connection to your town/ city, university, college, or department?) In order to help you figure out what can be done next—what you want to build or keep or tap into or even let go of—you might want to start with a purposeful look around.

You might want to look at your staff in the early part of this review. Who has joined you in this project and what do they bring, what are their lenses on the world?—and what is the position that you share and can take forward together? (More in Chapter 3 on using individual talents as well as opportunities with equity, diversity, and inclusion [EDI].) Knowing the ground you stand on together means being a little more certain about the intent, about moving into the future. You will need that momentum.

Literary journals are a lot of work—and can be a lot of fun when the work is for an agreed-upon purpose. While making a space to publish the words

The best thing we did in creating *Gandy Dancer* was make it a SUNY-wide publication. SUNY is the New York State University system and it includes 64 colleges, community colleges, and university centers. There were several local literary journals on our campus already, and we felt we needed to do something different. From that decision, came our mission and our name: *Gandy Dancer*. This is slang for the railroad workers who adjusted the tracks so trains could run smoothly. We like to think that we're working in that tradition, connecting readers and writers and artists across the state of New York.

—Rachel Hall, Faculty Advisor, *Gandy Dancer*, SUNY Geneseo

and ideas of other people is a laudable undertaking by itself, it has to be held together by a vision that members of the group can ascribe to. As wordsmiths often know, it may take more words, more attempts at getting it clear, in order to eventually revise and bring everyone along. Hang in there. Once you get busy investigating the moving parts presented in this chapter, keep your stated purpose in mind and remember that there are only so many hours in a day, so many things you can do at once. Plans taken to fruition might take longer than you think, might require more steps when the larger vision is taken into account—while other times the efforts click right into shape. It is fortunate when the end result turns out far greater than the sum of the parts. While you and your staff are taking/teaching classes and some staffers are holding down a job (or two), always recall that you can look around at what you have and celebrate the collective vision as the heart of the organization.

You, all of you, are the ones that make everything happen at your journal. When communicating with each other, you have to be thorough and honest. Each task going forward, including this initial investigation, takes time. (Leaving tasks to the last minute is rarely helpful—though writers are notorious for putting things off and being motivated by deadlines.) Being mindful of everyone's schedule and availability is key. Doodle polls, for instance, while helpful for meetings, can't solve the problem of everyone getting all their work done on time and showing up. You may need a regular weekly meeting time and a calendar of clear deadlines from the outset. And don't wait for perfection because it isn't showing up—or at least not on time. Students tend to understand the concept of schedules, so you have that in your favor. Everyone in your organization needs to know that schedules, in publications, are vital, because there can be a lot of people waiting for one thing to get done before the next thing can happen. And everyone should be encouraged to say what they can/can't do and when they can/can't do it—so as not to leave the others hoping and waiting. The staff you are working with—they are probably writers, too—is what you've got. Take their skills and interest as the most valuable asset of your organization. And respect the myriad ways they can show their commitment.

Our own magazine has a history dating back to 1917, but even if you are starting one this year, establish a tradition, build that tradition, and honor that tradition. This history can give the enterprise weight beyond a single department, garnering respect from other students, faculty, and administration.

—S. Craig Renfroe Jr., Faculty Advisor, *Signet* at
Queens University of Charlotte

Building a literary journal also means creating history, the written record of the moment. Your choice of voices, what you decide to publish in your journal, says a lot about you at that time in that place. People in the future will be able to access that vision when they read what you've produced. You will become a point in a line, a link in a chain. This is where creating your own mission statement can be helpful as a guide. The purpose of creating a journal must include the desire to see it continue and thrive after you have passed the duties to the next set of editors. Some level of continuity is necessary while new avenues must be opened when the situation and environment changes. (The recent pandemic has changed and will change a great deal of simple, assumed habits in our everyday lives. Likewise, the Black Lives Matter movement has provided the opportunity to get things moving, finally. Find the open door in the supposed chaos.) The bottom line is this: what you do has to be relevant to you first. You must sometimes dig a little deeper, look around a bit longer, to understand where you are and what you are doing and why.

A Journal with a History

If you are not starting from scratch, it may be very useful to get some background on what you have inherited. Look into the history of the organization, even the part that is not written down. Ask people—new faculty and older ones, for instance. Perhaps there are former editors living in the area. (You will get different stories, so the more people you ask, the clearer the picture should be.) There might even be former editors on the board (if you have one) or involved in local arts organizations. They would most likely appreciate your interest in their work at the journal and might be able to offer help or suggest connections for later projects and the specific needs you might face. Info-gathering (a type of networking, too) can be time-consuming, yes, but it's worth a lot when your instinct to ask is rewarded by a willing voice you've reached out to in the past. ("I remember you— I'd love to contribute to your fundraiser!" Who wouldn't love to hear that?) A journal that's been in place—even if you are reviving a journal that's been neglected for a while—certainly had a platform that could help you see a piece of the path forward for your vision, or at least prevent you from recreating the wheel. Who started the journal and why? Read past issues from a library archive and see what kind of work was published. Ask people their opinions about the journal and see what kind of reputation it gathered. You might find that your peers, the other student writers you see in classes or at readings, have a view of the journal that surprises you. (Or they might not even know it exists.) Things change, some things stay the same for a while, but it's all good information. Here are some questions you might consider investigating at the outset:

Basic Details

- **Who is involved in staffing the journal?**—students in the humanities and languages, or students from all parts of the university? Was the faculty involved in choosing editors or were student editors replacing themselves year to year?

- **The name of your journal—where did it come from?** Don't rename your journal without well-considered thought because you lose the power of history and easy identification. It could be helpful to understand the validity of the current name, or the complications of continuing with that name. If you do choose to rename your journal, choose carefully and with plenty of input from staff, faculty, students, board, and maybe administrators—the people who make the journal possible. The stakeholders.

- **Is there or has there been in the past an office space for the journal?**—or what might be available for storage, setting up a computer and printer, and holding meetings? You need a place to do your work.

- **Who is the faculty advisor and what is the level of their involvement?** Find out how this person is chosen and see if any present or former advisors are around to answer questions about past practices and the history of the journal.

- **Read a few past issues of the journal**—how does it strike you? What might you want to keep or dispense with? (See the next text box below.)

- **Has there been a traditional connection to other departments like Art, Computer Information Systems, Music, Theater, Business, or Communications?** And how can you maintain that connection going forward? Ask students, faculty, and staff who might have been around during the production phase of the journal in the recent past. Connections to these departments and others can be valuable when you want to put out the word for submissions or events, do layout, involve other students in design projects, get help with the business end, websites, social media, etc.

Paperwork

- **Where are back issues stored? Is there an online searchable archive?** Is there a print archive in the department or in the library? Don't throw old copies away—it's disrespectful of the work that went into producing the journal, and you never know when the poet or fiction-writer published in that issue might win a Pulitzer. (Believe me, it happens.) Find a secure place to store past issues, and be sure to ask at the library if there is an archive (or any interest in an archive) that you might be able to contribute to (see Chapter 2 for further discussion on library and institutional archives).

- **Does the journal have a handbook?** Ask around—there may be several versions of answers, old documents put aside, but as you move forward, you don't want to misrepresent what has come before. Plus, you can work with or against the details you find— the past can help you define the future (more in Chapter 3 on Handbooks).

- **Was (or is) the journal part of a registered student organization?** That is, connected to an office of student engagement or activities, usually a consortium of student-led groups or clubs funded by student fees—which every registered student pays every semester. (More on registered student organizations in Chapter 2.)

- **Is there an existing mission statement for your journal?** It might be in an existing handbook. If not, you might need to create one. A mission statement should be your organization in a nutshell: what you do, what you stand for, what you intend. Descriptive and declarative. Be sure to follow through.

Money

- **Was there (is there) a budget and who controls the money?** Where is the money kept (a school account housed where?) and how is it spent? Take a look at the books if you can get hold of them.

- **Who has funded the journal?** Has that funding stream changed in the last few years? How and why?

- **Where do you purchase your web hosting and domain name?** Who designed the website and who does the maintenance? What about existing contracts? Who printed the journal and was the organization required to get several bids for printing? (Has anyone recently looked around for printers in your area or maybe even printers in other states who specialize in small journals? More in Chapter 3.)

Looking Forward

- **Know who you are talking to—your greatest value is in your face-forward.** As you investigate the journal's history, be prepared to say something about your own vision for the journal when you talk to people. Be sure that it is a forward vision, not dismissal or disdain for what's gone before especially since the person in front of you might have contributed resources in the past.

- **Was another platform ever considered?** Whether the journal is print or online, how was that decision made?

- **Has the journal been in-house (submissions come from within the university) or have there been writers from all over the country, state, or local community published in the past?** Be absolutely clear on the parameters you are inheriting because you may have to ascribe to them in order to explain them to writers you contact about submitting their work OR you might need to update/ change the parameters and be very well informed about how those new changes effect the journal. Be aware of the former arguments.

- **Who has the journal been aimed at, what readership?** This is vital. If you have a small program and the readership is simply registered students, the readership could also be students considering your university for the study of literature or creative writing—in other words, the university Admissions Office might be able to connect your journal with future readers and editors. (Maybe they want to send you some money for those copies?) If the readership is wider, how did the staff reach those readers in the past? (Hint: the families of writers will often want to purchase several copies.)

Honor the work of others: remember that you are never alone. Other editors have gone before you, others will come after you, creating this journal or a related endeavor. Do not disparage what others have done. Find kind ways to say that you want to change from one mode of doing things to another—accentuate the positive rather than couching others' work as negative. Remember that someone else will be looking at *you* in the rear-view mirror someday. Do not assume that no one else has done anything new, thought about xyz, wanted to try something risky, committed to doing a "reasonable" thing then attempted to make changes and failed (or succeeded!). Be willing to learn and always remember that the work of publishing other peoples' writing is an honor. You are being trusted as others have been trusted before you. Exercise your humility and gratitude daily.

There are a million considerations when coming to an understanding of what you have in front of you with a literary journal that's been around for a while. But trust your impressions. What existing qualities are worth more attention? Make a list of the changes you want to make, the ideas you have for making adjustments. Prioritize. Talk to people about what you want to do going forward. And be reasonable—you can't do everything. You are going to be one in a long line (we hope) of editors and staff who have put their heart and soul into the structure and planning. Circumstances change constantly, so be generous, insightful—speak up!—and take risks with that list of priorities and don't be afraid to try a few drafts. Someone started this journal, after all, and someone else carried it forward to you. If the journal was recently started, remember: *how perfectly "professional" are the first efforts of anything?*

When you are collecting information on your literary journal, keep track of *all* your impressions. One detail here or there might come back to help you navigate a future decision. Here's an example: one of the things that can drive the physical appearance of the journal is the funding. Prettier products typically cost more. You might see that the journal has changed format a couple of times—ask around: why? (Probably funding. Maybe a passing donor.) Perhaps one of the journal's incarnations was particularly attractive and you find out that a faculty member in graphic design lent a hand by giving a graduate student some course credit for the redesign—carried forward for several issues because the InDesign file from the first issue of the redesign was easy to manipulate by the undergraduates on staff. Even if the journal moved away from that design, or has gone online, perhaps that faculty member in graphic design (or a related field) would be willing to give a current graduate student the opportunity to redesign the journal/website or update what you have.

When you are inheriting a journal and you have a lot of new ideas, do not change everything at once. Continuity, as already mentioned, matters. Recognition is important. If you simply slap the same title on a totally new product (or change the title and not the product, or both)—forgetting that reputation and connection are a part of the inherited wealth (in most cases, not all)—you will risk losing the respect and interest of those who have been

With the other editors, consider what the investigation into your journal has brought forward. Pitch ideas for change to each other and see what level of interest, enthusiasm, or disinterest there might be among staff members and why. Ask each other a lot of questions and be sure to go beyond your assumptions—it is very easy to shut down a line of investigation before it gets to the valuable pearl of thought. Keep talking.

Kalliope is Penn State's student literary magazine with roots reaching back to the first print journal published at University Park in 1939. After serving for several years as advisor to the club that publishes the journal each spring, I began in fall 2016 teaching a class with the goal of creating an online "sister" magazine to help move *Kalliope* and student writing into an online space. That first fall, students faced many bedrock decisions—what name would we use? What would our website look like? What and who would we publish? How would we promote and celebrate student work? The first students decided to give the journal a new (but related) Greek muse name (*Klio*), to brand it with a recognizable logo, to open submissions to all 24 Penn State Commonwealth Campuses, to feature writers and artists from past *Kalliope* print editions, to publish blog posts about the creative arts at Penn State, and to hold an in-person Art Jam, open to poets and musicians alike. They made all of these decisions after analyzing and presenting on an array of online literary magazines from around the world. Since its inception in 2016, *Klio* classes each fall have worked to build and improve on the previous class' work. For instance, we now have a Music Editor who curates a Soundcloud collection of Penn State musical artists. We've begun sharing poetry and interview podcasts, and are working toward featuring more multi-media work on our site.

— Alison Condie Jaenicke, Faculty Advisor, *Kalliope*
(print literary magazine) and *Klio* (online creative arts journal),
Penn State, University Park.

paying attention and are still invested. When you produce a new issue, you will be competing for the attention of readers and supporters both. But, who knows? It might be the right time for that risk.

Starting a New Journal

Starting a new journal is very exciting, but there is a lot of preparation work to be done. The above section on past support for an existing journal has given you some idea of the players involved in keeping a journal alive, but it also can give you an idea of who to ask for help in getting started. Below are a few ideas and questions to consider if you are going to be a founding editor:

- **What support is there in your home department?** Of course ask the faculty members who teach creative writing (and perhaps art or music), but ask the faculty members who sponsor other groups in your department—Sigma Tau Delta (English Honors Society),

Honors College, Shakespeare Reading Group, Comix Club, Improv—ask if they know of anyone (students or faculty) who might want to join a group of student editors to produce published creative work. Ask the chair of your department perhaps *after* you ask others, so you can report to the chair on the interest and commitments you have collected so far.

- Once you have a core group of people interested, **create a mission statement**. Look at the mission statements of other journals (you can find these online). What will make your journal special and attractive to the writers and readers you want to connect with?

- **Consider becoming a registered student organization** (an official student group housed within an office of student engagement and funded by student fees—see Chapter 2). This is a little work (signing up, training, maintaining records of officers) but it can give you a valuable structure and support—including access to student fees (for printing/hosting, events, travel to conferences, even editor stipends) as well as some help with banking (if they partner with a university credit union, for instance), events (cheap or free room reservations), and even office space. They may sponsor "get involved" events during the academic year, where you can find students who are looking for an opportunity to engage in a professional interest, like the experience you are offering, by applying the skills they have gained during their studies.

- **Devise a plan that you can present to those you talk with**: is this an in-house journal (publishing only students—and maybe staff and faculty—who attend your university) or is it regional or national or international? What size—how big of a print run and how many pages? What kind of website do you want? Who might the sponsors be? How many staff are needed? (And how many might you already have?) What would be your editorial process? How and when would you distribute the journal? You won't have all of these answers lined up, but as you read through this book and make some plans that you can commit to as objectives—and talk to people at your institution—you might discover that you have enough support and interest to start strong. When you ask someone for something, know that you are in the right place—do the research ahead.

- **Remember to be inclusive**. No doubt you have a variety of different writers at your institutions—as well as musicians and artists. Diversity adds value. Include the community of writers surrounding your institution, and the wealth grows. While you will be defining your journal in certain distinct ways, remember that you are only as strong as the support you get—and give. At initial planning, bring people in who can add to the strength of choices and ideas. Listen to their ideas and include their vision, too.

- **Look for faculty mentors.** This can be an official advisor through your department or college (who might even get a course release for helping you out) or through student government/office of student engagement system—or it can be unofficial, to start. There may be people who could help you navigate institutional offices/systems and negotiate with university offices that might have an interest in helping you get started. They might even have colleagues, people they work with on any number of other actions or committees from across the university, who would be helpful in putting out the word or setting you in the right direction. Don't be afraid to ask a lot of questions.

- **Be realistic about an online presence.** Look up the prices for web hosting and/or design software. Call that local printer and ask what a perfect-bound, eighty-page, 8.5 x 5.5-inch book would cost for 250 copies. Don't be discouraged—find another printer. Look at other online magazines for ideas. Consider starting with a very simple journal. (There are a lot of online journals you can look at for ideas—see Appendix A.) Whether you decide print or online, talk to the webmaster at your institution to see if (a) the journal's website could be housed on the university's website (or if they could electronically handle the submissions through a university server) or (b) what they would need from you in order for them to host a link to your journal on the official department/college/university web pages.

- **Have a few other journals in hand (or links you can send around) to illustrate what it is you are trying to do.** Some of the people you speak to may have limited experience with a literary journal, others might know very well what you are talking about and might have suggestions for other journals that you can also reference as examples. They may have recent copies of journals in their offices. Be very specific about what you see in the examples that would be relevant to your project.

- **Consider producing events and invite your supporters.** If your new journal wants to host a poetry slam, or simply an open mic night, writers will come. But you will have to advertise. Ask a couple of published writers (from the community or from your department) to headline the event. Community writers may join you if you reach out to arrange a cosponsored event. Get a local bar or restaurant to set up a mic and rearrange chairs on a slow night. Take the show to a university/college commons area during lunchtime or get a table at the student union and give out writing prompts in exchange for email addresses so you can tell everyone when and where the next event is taking place. (For more detail, see the section on "Reading Series and Other Events" in Chapter 5.)

- **Ask for funding.** (Say the word "money" out loud, repeatedly, in front of the mirror before you meet with a potential donor.) This one is hard for most writers. We are not a sales force, usually, and there's the introvert in us that typically wants to … do it alone. But you will need financial support, so get ready to ask for it. Have some realistic figures (the minimum) and dreamy ideas (the maximum you can imagine, with details and rationalization). If you get a "no," ask what it would take to get a "yes." Ask for other suggestions—who else might be able to fund this enterprise? Never take the answer personally. Perhaps someone can point you toward the person in the Development Office who can help you find someone to fund an endowment. This part can take some time, but if you don't start, your journal will never get there.

The items in the lists above certainly illustrate the most common moving parts of an undergraduate literary journal. Once you get going, it will become obvious how they all fit together. Do not misunderstand: you do not have to do all these things. And there are other things you could do instead. There may already be support in place at your college or university for arts projects—but you could always use more support, so take notes when people with some investment (faculty and administrators, but also people from local literary organizations) explain their views. Maybe there are new faculty members who haven't been asked to be involved yet. Hopefully you can imagine going forward with a sense of purpose once you have some knowledge about what's out there, what's been done, and what might be possible right now.

The bottom line, whether your journal is new or you are picking up the torch, is this: look around. Who do you want to be? What do you want to publish? What makes sense to publish? Where are you, what part of the country? (Look out the window: is that why the journal you inherited is called *Mountain Top*?) What is it *about* the landscape and the people that can actually contribute to the words on a page that you are going to honor with your hard work? What is right in front of you that you can use to build a brand for your journal, to connect it to the place and the people you want to reach?

When you are going through this discovery process, don't forget to look at who is sitting next to you in this endeavor. As was mentioned above, the students who show up each year to produce the journal will have everything to do with what happens. Again, what are *they* interested in doing? What skills do *they* bring to the endeavor? Since most literary journals at colleges and universities are run by student volunteers, you have to be realistic about the skills and the willingness (and the actual commitment, as opposed to the enthusiasm without follow-up) of your colleagues in this project. Everyone is bound to learn new things. You may be surprised to find that your poetry editor is very savvy with social media and the managing editor actually

Most students who run campus literary journals find that a lot of students at the institution have never heard of the journal. (Advertising will be covered in Chapter 2.) This is related to a similar problem that matches the perception of a closed system: the journal is run by a bunch of friends who might not welcome the input of others (at best) and might have a very narrow and unfair judgment of the other writers around them (the worst). As difficult as democracy is, a diversity of voices and viewpoints is essential if the journal is going to thrive. #1: Do not make assumptions about people. Instead, engage each other in a trade of information. Include a variety of people on staff and in your selections. Reach out. Editors have to be willing to work for a platform (your journal) that serves other people's voices. This is literary citizenship (covered later, in Chapter 5.) Along these lines, I suggest that no journal should publish the work of the editors. Just don't do it—or if you do, get ready for the eye rolls and backlash. (One caveat: very, very small schools with a handful of creative writers might need to build a different kind of journal—and publish some work by the staff.) And if possible, someone on your staff—as many people as possible on staff—should actively welcome newcomers and encourage everyone on staff to offer their opinions and ideas concerning problem solving and decision making. It can be a hard balance to include every voice and yet make decisions that are not just common denominator. A friendly reach from "the journal" toward the people you encounter (you want them to submit their work, read the journal, and/or attend an event) will make a huge difference in your ultimate success. Don't be nervous, be kind and inviting. Keep the staff's inside jokes to closed meetings.

interned with a Certified Public Accountant (CPA). The co-managing editor is willing to learn about WordPress. You may have a slush-pile reader who knows InDesign. The trick here is to make sure that people don't overcommit, overschedule, and burn out. Be realistic—and be kind. Everyone is trying to get all their work done—and some might need regular reminders. Each year, each issue, will be different. The process will be different. It will reflect the people who did the work, and that is you.

Consider Your Format/Platform

Well, the obvious question is this: what do you want to publish? Before you even consider your format, consider what it is you want to deliver to readers: what is the aesthetic of your journal? (What *kind* of poetry, fiction, nonfiction, art, music, reviews, graphics do you want to include? What is the level of commitment to artwork, for instance, or music or performance?)

The "aesthetics" questions can be a hard question for most students who are just learning to identify the aesthetic of texts they are reading in their literature classes or the art objects they are studying in an art history course. The terms used to describe an aesthetic can seem academic, but they are useful for communicating intent. You need to know how they apply to you.

Most new editors will likely say "We want to publish good stuff!" While that goes without saying, it will not help you tell the writers submitting their work if they are submitting the appropriate work to the appropriate journal. Everything has an aesthetic—it's time to start recognizing the fact. Not easy, but you want to tell the writers (and to some extent the readers) what to expect. Plus, you will have to post guidelines for submissions (more on that in Chapter 3). If you can define the aesthetic in terms that are as specific as possible, couched in the positive ("we are looking for short lyrical essays") and not the negative ("no sci-fi or fantasy or romance") you will have an easier time considering which descriptive words to choose. "We publish realist literary fiction … " or "We are interested in speculative writing and absurdist art in a variety of formats as well as graphic poetry and black-and-white photography … " You get the picture, right? Try to spell out the past or present (or future) aesthetic so you can spell out your own. (Not everyone on staff has to have the same personal aesthetic—they simply have to recognize and use the journal's aesthetic.) An aesthetic might be hard to pin down, but it will save you a lot of time going forward if you can be clear about your vision. And don't go too narrow, or you won't get submissions. To some extent your aesthetic will help you choose a format, though not necessarily or obviously. You can easily put audio and video files online. Printed volumes can have foldouts. Design options and costs—concerning websites or print magazines—may, however, overwhelm your thinking on which to choose. Budgets will often push you in one direction or another, plus what you already have available (web hosting or a printing shop) at your institution.

> It's important for a journal to have a recognizable "brand." At *Copper Nickel*, the work we often want to publish has something to do with socio-historical context. We also publish translation folios in every issue, along with a statement from the translator, to give context. You read *The Southern Review*, the aesthetic is often traditional narrative; at *Jubilat* you find more experimental, surreal work. It's important to think about your specific, recognizable identity. Wayne Miller, Professor and Editor-in-Chief, *Copper Nickel*—University of Colorado Denver.

When considering the aesthetic in relation to the format of your university literary journal, there are two obvious issues: (a) are you going to have a print journal or an online journal? and (b) are you going to be an in-house journal (only students at your institution can be published) or will you take submissions from the wider world? You can always do both in a variety of patterns. There will be a lot of opinions on what you should be doing, and it never hurts to try one thing and adjust according to result, but there are a few clear choices to consider when you start with your journal's aesthetic. For instance, if you are going to ask music students to submit audio files for your print journal, you will either have to burn a lot of discs (which can be done, even though they are going out of style) or go with an online format where you can easily post audio files. (You might need a production person for video and/or audio files.) Or you can do a mix: print your journal with some material and refer readers to a website for other material. Or have your print journal be a "best of" the online, regular journal. (Then the question becomes how often to do a "best of." If the answer is annually, that suggests at least four online issues per year mined for the top picks—a total of five "publications" in a year. Be sure to do your math.) You can limit your print journal to local submissions and open the online submissions to regional, national, or international writers. You might consider online for shorter texts and put longer works in a print edition. There are so many things you can do, and these will be driven by what you want and what you have. (Easy to say; harder to make the decisions.) If you start with a clear intention to publish a certain kind of work (you can't be an expert on everything—choose what you know and what interests you) everyone will have a lot easier time finding solutions for the best presentation format. Once some decisions are made, it's a lot more fun going forward.

Obviously, when you are starting out, start simple (you can also have a clearly defined plan to roll out later changes for future issues). I can't emphasize this enough: if you try to do too many things, none of them will be done well. Keep your focus on the quality of the work you want, along with a short list of realistic goals toward production. (Get out your calendars. How much time do you need to collect submission, process them, edit, do layout, proofread, and get the journal to the printer—who will also have a schedule? More on this in Chapter 3.) There are obvious pros and cons to online and print, but your situation will be particular. The standard in the literary world has been, of course, the print journal, and a lot can still be said for the quiet, singular item that you can take with you anywhere. But websites are growing in popularity, are generally cheaper, and it's very likely you can find a student who can put together a website on WordPress using one of their simple templates.

Print Journals

A print journal has been the usual form for undergraduate literary journals in recent decades. (In the way back, it was sometimes mimeograph, stapled.) Print has a lot of advantages for student groups: when it's done it's done (no further maintenance of a website—it exists as long as someone can put a hand on a copy). Also, designing the item, the artifact (choosing art, paper, cover design, fonts, layout options) can be fun. (It can also be a pain if you don't have someone who is either versed in a software program like InDesign or someone who is willing to dive in and learn—fast. Again, more on production in Chapters 3 and 4.) Being able to hand someone a copy of what you've put together is another way of saying "read this"—a print journal has a presence and does not disappear with a click, does not demand more screen time. Writers tend to keep copies of their published work, and some will appreciate the artifact with their name on it. A well-designed book is comfortable to hold and beautiful pages are a pleasure to share, to slip into your backpack or to loan to a friend.

Print is also expensive. You can sell copies of a print journal to help defray the cost, but it is rare for sales to equal printing costs (which are at minimum $5 a "book"). Copies can be given to staff and to contributors—a reward for their work. Family and friends buy copies too—people want to celebrate the writer's success at being published, for instance. (Don't price copies so high that they don't sell at all.) Storage for back copies is usually a question—your university or college probably has a closet somewhere, you hope—and if you have an issue that sells out you might have to do a second printing. Or your printer might do on-demand printing. You also have to keep track of what you have in stock, and where the print run went (to whom, when, etc.—so that you can make better guesses for next time). Send a couple of copies to the dean who committed funding to your project—and another few to the chair of the department—and how many go to the Admissions Office? Do contributors get one copy or two? Someone has to keep track.

Since there are hundreds of student literary magazines all across the country, you might receive orders for your magazine from students who are doing exactly what you are doing right now: figuring out how to put together a journal by looking at the existing journals out there. Or they might be in a creative writing class that requires students to report on a student journal and/or submit their work to one. Subscriptions might be possible, but that means another job for someone, tracking the subscriptions and figuring out when/how to ask for renewals. Again, it can easily be set up, but someone has to do it and maintain it.

Undergraduate print journals are published, on average, once or twice a year—following the semester/term calendar for meetings and production deadlines. Some, as previously mentioned, are connected to a publication practicum course. There are also schools with multiple undergraduate journals, like Emerson and Susquehanna—each with a separate focus, purpose, and organization or staff—and some institutions offer a degree in editing/publishing. Some journals also work alongside a schedule of awards or prizes—also used to help pay for printing. So there is some flexibility with print, but the more it is attached to other entities like a degree program, a course, or a student organization, there may be an expectation that it follow guidelines *not* established by the staff.

One final note on print journals: who will know what you are, where you are, how to submit, if you don't have a website? If you have a print journal, let's face it, you will also need a website. Basic information, a link to the submission manager (mostly Submittable these days), a list of what's coming up or what happened with that contest you ran last year ... and archives. A website is necessary. Once your website is up and running, it can be more or less sophisticated, and you will face the inevitable question of how it supports the journal. How about putting a few poems up there to represent the best of the most recent print journal? Maybe a student musical performance—an audio file? (Some magazines use QR codes for audio files—a reader can then download the audio file rather than have it hosted on the website.) Inevitably you may have to consider: is it simply better to publish your next issue online?

Online Journals

The best thing about online journals is that they can be accessed from anywhere as long as you have a phone, tablet, or computer. Most writers do. The worst thing about online journals is that someone has to be paying attention all the time. Posting, arranging, monitoring security issues (this is the short list), paying the bills—you need a committed and really sharp web editor. At least one. There has to be continuity—also known as maintenance and updating. An outdated or messy website will make a reader (or writer) move on and not return. A well-designed and maintained website can present the reader with just enough choices to get their attention and keep them clicking from page to page, looking for more gems, poetry to fiction to nonfiction to art and music or performance and back again for the next issue. And then there is the mobile site. If no one is paying attention, websites do get hacked, crash, etc.

More and more, people are comfortable reading online. It's not true of everyone, but we are all, generally, doing more reading online than in print. There's a general claim that no one likes to read longer works online, but the publishers of a lot of high-profile, online magazines (or print magazines that also put features online) and the whole tablet reader industry will refute this. If the material is compelling, you don't have to use only the shortest poems and stories for web pages. (Again, what is your aesthetic?) If you are tending toward the online choice, remember that people also read on their phones, so you must be sure that your mobile site is also attractive and easy to use for people reading longer works.

Artwork can look really stunning online, much better than on the printed page, unless you can afford fantastic paper and the color pages. You can make web pages with only text (and you can include downloadable PDFs, though there are other considerations there—for instance, paging through and downloading), but there is still the design of the page. Homepages look better with attractive visuals (even if you don't "publish" artwork). You can find free graphic material online, but the search for open-source images can take a lot longer than looking through art submissions. Still, the design element is something to consider because just like print, website styles change over time and someone will want to consider updating your theme now and then—if not the hosting.

Online journals can be published more frequently than print. They can include fewer or more pieces without seeming hugely different (more flexibility to extend to your staff). More issues per year with lower total word counts can make your slush pile a little less stressful, if you are good at keeping up—though you can have a more humane, constantly processing slush pile system for a print journal, too. (Clearing the decks of every last submission once or twice a year is typical for undergraduate print journals.) There is simply a wider range of easy choices with online journals. You can try things without a lot of investment in the outcome. For instance, if the pieces to be published are chosen, edited, and ready, and you have a willing web editor, you can publish during the summer months when your readership (other students, perhaps) might have more time to check it out. Keep track of the views.

More and more, writers are submitting to online journals, perhaps in part because their pieces are always a few clicks away—easily available, free to everyone. You don't have to dust off a book and hand it to your cousin. Writers can send someone the link or print out the pages. Almost all submissions are now done online—there are a few holdouts, and some universities might still prefer an in-house and paper-based process, but there is no doubt that on the professional end, journals have websites and online submission procedures. Institutions might like the online format better because it is paperless and easier for alum and prospective students to access. The product of your education is right there. This might put a little more pressure on your editorial staff to publish work that the institution will not frown upon ("Can we honestly publish this hilarious essay about the biology of poop?") but questions like that can be worked out in a discussion with your advisor.

Online journals still have expenses too, of course—and one of those, now, is security software or an upgraded (more expensive) hosting package with security measures included. No one wants to lose a whole website to a hacker (usually bots) or a ransomware attack. (Honestly, you are not, as a literary magazine, exactly a prime target—but your university might be; if your magazine is on their site, it is reasonable to ask about security measures.) You also need computer terminals if you are producing an online journal. Most of your staff members will already have laptops, probably, but you might be well served to have an office computer powerful enough to handle big files quickly—and store them for everyone's access (like on

If your journal is open to students across the university, you may very well find students in Art who can help you find some valuable student art to use online or on the printed page. A Communication department might have students who run a radio station or maybe there's a specific student interested in producing podcasts. Music? You can post files (audio or video) on your website that feature student musicians. You might have a short clip of a poet reading a poem at a recent reading. If your institution has a computer center or a business college, you have a chance to find IT students who want to practice what they are learning, too. Interviews? There is probably a sound booth somewhere. A business college probably includes degrees in marketing, information systems, business practices for nonprofits—you might find all the help you need close by.

Google Drive or on the server at your institution). When your new web editor arrives, because the trustworthy comrade who was your previous web editor graduated, you want them to have access to everything they need to pick up where the last web editor left off.

In-House or International—or Anything in Between

As a student-run organization, you might have some leeway to make your own decisions about the scope of your journal, but this is not always the case. Often this question is answered by the university and it has to do with funding. Some institutions, especially when they commit student fees to a literary journal, will require that your journal feature student writers and only students presently registered at your university. (Or maybe students, staff, faculty, and alum—or some combination of these.) This is because those student fees might be earmarked to promote the work of the students who pay the fees. Not a bad idea. You can argue your point to the appropriate committee (for or against in-house only), and in this uber-connected world you might win the argument (pointing out that the university and the students might want to include connections to the community, or not— local, regional, national, even international, or not), but go in with evidence and a clear request, reasonable language, and a lot of patience. A change might take several university entities signing on to an agreement. (Literally or figuratively.) Colleges and universities can move slowly.

There is usually some departmental oversight of student literary magazines (English Department, or Languages, or Humanities, Cultural Studies—departments have been changing name and shape for the last couple of decades and will continue to do so). Ask questions. It's good to know what's in place—or to know the landscape so you can work toward what you want without wasting time. Remember this: if someone wants a say in what is done, they really should help pay for the journal or support it in a meaningful way. The places you might go for funding, if no one else is willing to help pay for your journal, might be the college (the college being the collection of departments that would be most appropriate—usually the Humanities or the Arts or maybe even an Honors program). Or, next stop, the Provost's Office. The Provost is the chief academic officer at a university (in other words, the head of the faculty which means the head of all the colleges). Most Provosts pay a lot of attention to what students produce—it's called "outcomes." If you have a proposal that the department and college have not been enthusiastic about, and a registered student organization is not possible, perhaps you can present your ideas to the Provost. Again, look at the university's mission statement before you ask to talk to the Provost and have a good argument concerning your student-centered and student-run, extracurricular (if it's not part of a publishing course) activity.

Does your university have a press? By that I mean publishing group, not a printing concern—though some universities have that, too. It's quite probable that other units (departments, colleges, programs, etc.) are publishing journals or books or maintain professional websites. Some larger universities have university presses which house all these publishing groups together (for good or naught—but the argument is usually the sharing of resources). You might try seeing if support is available there, especially if you are required to be a completely in-house journal. These other journals might also lend professional (and institutional) advice.

There are benefits to in-house publications: focusing on the home talent is not a bad idea. (Publishing just your friends, however, is not great, as I point out several times in this book.) The pool of submitters is very clearly defined, plus other elements of the work are surrounded by whatever limits to resources you encounter. (If you have to use an in-house print shop, you are going to be limited by what they can do.)

You can usually convince institutional communication offices to get the word out ahead of a submission deadline and to promote a launch or advertise a prize. You may be very surprised by the wider institutional support you get with an in-house journal. You will get an opportunity to meet people from other departments who share your interest in creative writing and other arts. Publishing students at your school also gives everyone, from every department, a chance to come together and celebrate *writing*. (Administrators love that.) When the journal is launched (made available, whether print or online) bringing everyone together for a reading and celebration is also another way to get attention for your project and to hear about what other people think of the result. If you do such an event, let the Office of Admissions know and they will appreciate the fact that visiting students could be invited to attend.

If you are looking for more submissions to choose from, you can open up your submissions manager to writers in the area (the county, the state), the

A note of caution here about funding. University entities that might fund your project will probably have only a short list of things they will pay for. (If you are handed some $ and are told to go spend it—no reporting back, no strictures—that would be amazing!) An office of student engagement (or Registered Student Organization Office) might require you to submit a budget, for instance, or maybe a report at the beginning and end of the year. In other words, funding is usually not "free"—and might also have an expiration date. Always ask what the parameters are to whatever gift or offer or account is in place. (Spell out the parameters you *want* on any gift/favor you are asking for. And be flexible.) All universities have to account for what they are given (donations) and how they spend that money. More on this later, but you can also do some fundraising—this is how nonprofits endure. (Brick and mortar universities are mostly nonprofits, whether private or public. If you are at a *for-profit* university, parts of this might be similar, but by definition you can be sure that they are not giving away money.) There are all kinds of in-kind donations (rooms, computer/printer, event space) that will also work for your journal. Again, ask questions and be clear about what you want and why, and ask polite questions about what exactly is being offered.

country, or invite writers from all over the world. Once you move beyond the boundaries of your college or university, you have a lot of choices to make. It is not necessarily more "professional" to open up your journal to the world of letters, but if you do, you should understand what landscape you are entering. There is a lot of competition, a ton of writers, and several "generally accepted practices" (discussed mostly in Chapter 3 and Chapter 4) for Calls for Submissions, processing the slush pile, accepting and rejecting pieces, and working with writers you want to publish. You could get slammed with material you don't necessarily want. (See "aesthetics" earlier in this chapter.) In either case—in-house or international—you have to be clear and communicate effectively and respond reasonably. There is, however, more at stake professionally for a journal that's open to the general public. If your journal has (or wants) recognition from the larger literary world, then you have to be sure it deserves that recognition. It will take time to build that reputation, as well. In the quest to become a national journal (or maintain that status), let's say, you have to safeguard your ongoing reputation by not letting things fall through the cracks—by not answering your email for months at a time, let's say, or by neglecting to post your next issue on time. And, again, you must be clear on the rules and processes when you ask for submissions, and you must follow all of those rules yourself (see Chapter 3).

Journals that include writing from the wide world may have the advantage of getting "better" writing—or at least different kinds of writing, and writing from professionals if you want professional writers competing with newbies (or not—some national undergraduate literary journals only publish undergraduates, from any university, or they only publish writers who have not attended graduate school in creative writing or writers without published books). But those journals also have to be honest with the public about what they are exactly looking for—this goes back to knowing your aesthetic and being able to define it and include it in guidelines so you don't end up with a lot of submissions that are from people who are throwing darts (submitting everywhere just because they can) and have obviously never read your journal. If you are going for a broader audience, that's great. (Have mercy on your slush pile readers.) But you also have to consider the subject matter that a broader audience brings and choose writing that is not just about being a kid or a college student. Believe me, you will get all kinds of writing. With fresh eyes, you might find something in your slush pile from a writer on another continent that is truly unique to your slush pile readers (then they have to agree on it), or perhaps you will find a piece that no one else has been willing to publish but your staff finds it … remarkable! This is true of art, essays, poems, stories, graphic writing, reviews, and interviews. You never know what might show up, and this can be quite fun but also daunting.

Journals that take risks and invite a broader view also bring attention to your institution, and your advisors will be aware of this. "How do we look?" Are you actually representing, in what you publish, the wide variety of work that is submitted? I'm not suggesting that you publish a representative sample of what is submitted, but I am suggesting that what is submitted will be a function of how you represent yourself, including how you run your journal and what you choose to print. One feeds the other, both ways. If you go the international submissions route, you might track

The question of "What is the criteria for which pieces get published?" is always difficult. It can make people more comfortable to believe that there are pieces which are objectively better than others rather than to sit with a piece in ambiguity and subjectivity. It's helped me to remember that a lot of what I think of as objective quality is merely my own subjective reaction, and the same is true for my colleagues. It feels like a more honest interpretation of the publishing process. What gets published is one group's interpretation of what they want to share, not one group deciding what is worthy. Plus our subjective preferences are always changing and growing…. John Lyons, Drama Editor (2020–2021), *earthwords: the undergraduate literary review*, University of Iowa.

down the international programs office at your university, and see, also, if anyone is taking students on international education adventures focused on creative writing. Are they connecting with writers in that country? Ask them to submit! Perhaps you, too, could make a connection with undergraduate journals in other countries (via email, perhaps) and get the opportunity to publish some very interesting work that simply isn't available nearby.

One last thing to consider about having an online and/or print publication: perhaps the print publication is for the university and the online publication is general public? Or the other way. Maybe your print version is a once-a-year themed issue. Your website could have a theme whenever you choose—being a little more flexible and swift. The online magazine could address current issues. You could have two separate journals each with its own purpose. As you can see, there are a lot of options. Now, may I point you back to the beginning of this chapter: look around. What do you already have? What do you want to do, who do you want to be (who are you already?), and where exactly do you want to go? Before you go much further with planning your time at the journal, you need to know what you've got—and have a pretty good idea of what is even possible going forward. Always, always, be patient (supporters change, financial landscapes rise and fall) and be very clear when communicating your ideas.

W hen doing an environmental scan of your university, don't forget to think about how campus events such as poetry slams can be easily filmed as part of an online publication. We have also used the Writing curriculum to capture and develop content created in coursework, enlivening a sense of audience for student writers. Campus-wide, we have partnered with organizations such as the Black Student Union, encouraging them to use the literary magazine as a means of amplifying campus presence. My advice? Don't think about reinventing the wheel. Think about using what is already working well to assemble a foundation—Amy Persichetti, Faculty Advisor, *The Woodcrest Magazine*, Cabrini University

Since you are, after all, an undergraduate literary magazine, you do not exist in a vacuum. You might have to lift your head from the work on occasion and look around. What else is going on at your university? See any potential new partners? Be ready to reach out—or to respond when someone else reaches out. Remember that you are part of a learning community. You might offer support to a student who wants to establish an open mic on Monday evenings in the dining hall. Go to that student recital or theater event and post a blog about it. These are your arts fellows. Offering a thank you (a postcard or a mention online or the dedication of the next issue) to

We have designed our literary magazine to function as the centerpiece of our Writing program. Students who are developing pieces in other classes can submit to the literary magazine (in addition to the campus-wide community). We run the production of the literary magazine as a class, which not only legitimizes expenses to administrators, but provides built-in advisory oversight by an experienced faculty member—Amy Persichetti, Faculty Advisor, *The Woodcrest Magazine*, Cabrini University

someone who has helped—a department chair for offering money or space, for example, or a donor who gave a one-time gift of a thousand dollars. This is so very important to the next chair and the next donor. And this also gives you an opportunity to see new and different avenues for connection, development, and change.

Know who you are—and show up for your fellow artists and writers because you *see* them. If you are a writer starting out, create an organization that supports other new artists. Know your audience and surprise them with how well you know them, by printing challenging material and beautiful work. And remember that your time with this journal—a student journal—at this university you have chosen and has chosen you, is limited. Make the best of it.

2

Financial Health, Viability, and Partnerships

What Type of "Business" Is a Literary Magazine?

A literary journal is a labor of love, as they do not tend to make money. The value is there, no doubt about it: they influence literary agents and small publishers who are looking for the newest writers and artists, the exciting trends. Still, in general, when money comes into play the stoutest and most determined editors (student or professional) take pause. You have to pay the bills. And while a lot can be done with a little, much can be wasted as well. I've seen undergraduate literary magazines exist on less than a thousand dollars a year. (Not too long, though; if you keep that up you probably have other means of support that are not evident in the same way as cash.) At the other end of the spectrum are magazines supported by massive endowments, like *Poetry*.

On average, the more established and successful university literary journals have budgets of 100K+ (not counting salaried staff, TAs, and faculty) and they probably have networks that non-academic-affiliated literary journals would be thrilled to keep. All professional literary journals exist (in large part or for periods of time) on volunteer/unpaid labor and a good name. A few well-known journals exist as an arm of book-publishing houses. Look up Red Hen Press and the *Los Angeles Review*. Most professional journals pay contributors. You can always be sure that literary agents read these journals—the best known journals perform the important function in the literary publishing industry of introducing new writers while also publishing new short-form works (also reviews and artwork and interviews) by established writers. The editors might be addressing a specific market (with a specific aesthetic or demographic in mind), or the journal might be attached to a related nonprofit such as a hospital (narrative medicine) or a group of writers and artists self-identifying (such as LBGTQ+). All these journals serve the industry, by which I mean writers and artists as well as other publishers, large and small. See *The Gay and Lesbian Review*.

Undergraduate journals have an opportunity to do new things as well, perhaps because they are monitored only by a department or program. They are lower stakes. As such, there can be innovation. They primarily provide professional experience—which is priceless. In the best case, student editors discover what excellent stewards they are of other peoples' work. Student journals also might come and go, and start again, publish twice a year and then once. And then back to twice. While money isn't the point, almost always the decisions on how to proceed have something to do with funding plus a willing, motivated and devoted staff.

Bottom line, you will have to manage money very carefully and be cautious with your spending—and be mindful of the value you really do offer. Rarely do student journals pay writers. (University of Houston's *Gulf Coast*, run by graduate students as a stand-alone nonprofit, is an exception: they have a board who does the fundraising and provides a lot of in-kind support.) Simply put, literary journals depend on an economy that is not based only in the monetary realm, but on support offered in-kind (services donated) or outside of the cash economy. For instance, if I own a gift shop I can donate items for your silent auction. Later, you might allow my employee to attend your poetry workshop for free. This is sometimes referred to as a "gift economy" (where things are traded and/or donated) or an "arts economy" (based in exposure and cultural trade). Consider that if you need a venue and I own a restaurant, I might host your organization for events (and maybe even provide food at reduced cost) and I might get more return patrons as a result. Students who would consider running an undergraduate journal, however, should be aware of the systems (not just academic, but real world) under which they operate: the nonprofit sector, for example. In our daily lives there are a huge number of cultural trades we agree to and act upon without even thinking—like changing our clothes so we don't smell or driving on the proper side of the road. Understanding your journal's cultural and economic position can help keep your journal alive and thriving by understanding and effectively using these other layers of cultural trade.

First, the gift economy. It is basically a barter system. You do someone a favor and they will do you or someone else a favor, and etc. on and on. Eventually, it is assumed, everyone gives and everyone gets. For instance, you invite local writers to be featured at one of your readings, and one of those writers may later suggest you be invited to a literary festival where your student editors get to network with publishers in your area, state, or region at a book fair. After a lively conversation about favorite writers your editors are invited to submit their work to a journal that has an interesting themed issue coming up (maybe they need more submissions on the topic).

Or, after you publish a particular writer who continues on with publishing, they may remember you and contribute a box of their newest book for a fundraiser. You invite other arts organizations to your events and they invite you to theirs. Networking happens. There are thousands of ways the give-and-take of the gift economy works in literary publishing, particularly journal publishing, and what drives it is love for the literary arts. Everyone recognizes the donated time and sweat as necessary for the literary enterprise to continue. However, do remember this: the gift economy is a wide circle and the trades are most frequently not crystal clear and not always efficient. Many people have exhausted themselves and their resources by giving a lot, frequently. These are donors and volunteers. Other magazines have gone under by taking plenty and not being generous to others. All these efforts are regularly traded and loosely tracked. If you aren't sure about your gift, or the give-and-take, ask around for feedback, gently.

Think wisely about what you have and what you need. Give according to your actual spare resources (extra pages for ads at the back of your journal, for instance) and only ask according to what you know others have. With university backing, you have a wealth of support simply as a part of an established institution. (Perhaps your department pays for mailing. Your Honors College may have a budget for student initiatives. Is there an English Honors Society in your department? You certainly have a captive

Student editors frequently wonder if they might publish their own work. I advise against—emphatically: "If you do that, it looks like you are here for your own gain and to help out your friends. The visuals are terrible—you will lose credibility, trust, and helpful relationships." Avoiding shameless self-promotion, these days, is less common, unfortunately. (Notice that your creative writing teachers don't assign their own books for their classes, not if they have any scruples.) Student literary magazines are often fueled by funds that are freely given to help students learn about editing—so they can make a platform for other writers. The purpose is to bring writers in. The university or college experience is about learning, and in this case you may have to learn how to be a good leader or team player and focus on the magazine, not your own pretensions for your creative work in the literary realm. You may lose student editors because of this policy (some students will want to submit more than they want to volunteer their time), but the editors you do get—and don't forget yourself, as a writer—will learn so much more about publishing by publishing the work of people you/they do not know. It will be worth the effort, *even in service to your writing*. I've known more upper editors at student literary journals who went on to publish successfully after their editing stints than I can possibly count. (See "Literary Citizenship" mentioned in Chapter 5.)

audience when it comes to recruiting new staff: faculty in your department may be happy to have you come in for a class visit.) Look carefully and be ready to "trade." Be generous to your local arts organizations who might not have a large institution supporting their reason for existence. Don't hang yourself out on a limb, of course. And remember the trades are not always immediate. Don't get disappointed when no one seems to notice. Do remember what you've given and what you've gotten. You don't want to feel stung because you gave your time and effort away, or because no one cares for what you offer.

The arts economy is not much different from the gift economy, trading as it does in "things" that aren't always money. So the arts economy as I'm referring to it here is based specifically in skills and materials. (Money is also in the mix for the arts economy: there are some hard truths in the arts about the bottom line. I'm simply addressing here the part that is not cash.) Visual artists, musicians, actresses/actors and theaters, writers, curators, production teams—none can exist without the others. This is cultural invention. Artists develop, for instance, by doing and (we hope) enjoying the creative tasks. If they become experts they might get hired—to write some music, do lighting, manage a venue, appear in a film, etc. In the case of literary publishing, an undergraduate editor might find an internship at a box office for a chamber group where they end up writing the playbill notes, discovering how much they love reviewing events. Publishers everywhere need art work and graphic designers, maybe even musicians for a fundraiser, theater people for readings—and the graphics people, musicians, and theater folks always need writers. (As a student, you get to try things.) The list of potential trades (and their rising value as an artist hones his/her/their craft and fosters personal presence in an arts community) is endless. Put yourself out there and see what you find. The key here, again, is to accurately assess what you have to offer and what you are asking for or accepting from some else—and what should be paid for. (There is plenty that you deserve to be paid for.) A little bit of the showman and operator exists in all artists (after all, art is self-expression on display); an extreme version of what I'm addressing here is the person everyone agrees is driven to succeed, the ambitious sort. That person may understand the arts economy very well by having a well-developed sense of who needs what, what should be given, what's available for their gain, and what should be paid for.

The point of the gift economy is that you simply give back somewhere, sometime, and likewise get an opportunity to receive at some point. Sometimes we call this good literary citizenship. We've all met writers and artists who are a bit awkward—people you invite to read who show up, bring no one with them, read their work, and leave without listening to the other readers. It's not polite, and people notice. Maybe they've merely had a bad day or perhaps they make a habit of discounting other people's attention. When we talk about literary citizenship (it's a thing these days—see Chapter 5), we are talking about people who do give back, who find a way to contribute to the literary economy (as unpaid editors of student literary magazines, for example). The arts economy may be that kind of economy as well, but you might have more of a direct trade situation in the arts economy: you design this for us and we will post your design business logo on our website. You write lyrics for this music and I will give you credit on my album. For a student literary magazine, there is a lot of potential in both economies and lots of excellent real-world lessons about the nonprofit world in both. For more on the topic of literary publishing and the various sorts of publishers and literary arts concerns active now, as well as a bit of history, take a look at *Literary Publishing in the 21st Century*, a collection of essays on the topic edited by Travis Kurowski, Wayne Miller, and Kevin Prufer.

The nonprofit sector—a large group of organizations that are not only arts based but found across the social spectrum—is probably where you are standing right now. Colleges and universities, public and private, are usually nonprofits. Nonprofits are organizations designed to provide some sort of service or research; they don't make money; they also don't pay taxes and are monitored for their activities to make sure they stick to their nonprofit, public service mission. So, your magazine that is housed at a college or university is essentially an arm of a nonprofit organization. Your magazine is certainly a not-for-profit enterprise, even if you are managing to get paid (a stipend, perhaps, paid by student fees)—because it is a learning opportunity. If you do get a stipend, you are not being paid for your time as an 'employee' (nonprofits can pay employees, but they don't try to make a profit *per se*, other than to cover costs) as most stipends for student editors go toward tuition costs. Whether or not you get a stipend, no college or university would (or should) ask you to *make* money. (Fundraise to cover costs, okay, yes.) You provide a service for the nonprofit, the university: a public platform for literary work.

Back to managing the journal's funds. Most departments have a money person who can explain university budgets/accounts to you, at least in general terms, and you might find out where all kinds of monies at universities come from and go to and why—just by talking to the right people. At least enough to inform you about the system at your institution. Visit the Accounts Payable office at your college or university and get the paperwork you need to present to printers (or any other business owner you buy services or materials from) so you are not charged sales tax. (Nonprofits have IRS paperwork that shows they are registered as tax exempt.) Your college or university may also have a Development Office that can help you with grants—internal and external. "Development Office" is the current term for "fundraising" at most universities. In other words, the university may or may not want to help you find money, since they probably have a lot of people already asking them for help finding some money somewhere. But it's worth asking, worth giving them a few copies of the journal, leaving your contact info, asking some questions. For instance, they might have already gotten a grant—it's quite possible—that you might benefit from. Someone

Find out everything you can about the material structure of how your journal is produced: Who funds it? Who prints it? This is just as important as your creative vision, if not more so. Putting a journal together can be a struggle between editors and their faculty advisor, and demystifying how everything works takes away someone's power to tell you "We can't do what you want with the journal because of [x reason about funding that you can't disprove]." Being ignorant of the material reality behind your journal can easily prevent you from implementing the aesthetic you want. "Thus do many calculations lead to victory, and few calculations to defeat," like they say on *The Sopranos*.
—Noah Mazer, *Gandy Dancer* Managing Editor 2018–2019

might have given money for inter-department student-based art projects, for example. Ask—and check back in case something new comes up.

So the good and bad news, to start, is this: as a nonprofit "business" you are not expected to make money, but you must be responsible with what you have, raise, earn, trade, or are given. That takes accounting.

The Budget

Of course you should always fit your financial expectations to the money you know you have—that's basic budgeting. You can always pursue further funding (more on fundraising in a moment) but it's best to make plans only for what you currently have or need. Cover the most important things first: your publishing or hosting costs. There may be money forthcoming from an office at the university, or a donor, but always be very certain that the money is, actually, happening—and perhaps have a plan B. At any rate, a budget helps you plan—and can help you with asking for more money, later, when you can show that you've been responsible with your resources. (Your predecessors can show you their budgets, hopefully, as a template.)

The most basic way of writing down a budget is simple: list your revenue and your expenses. Income can be listed by where it came from, expenses by where the money went. Here is an example that leaves a margin of roughly $1000 or about 1/7th of total expenses, as a cushion:

Expenses

Web hosting and domain	170
Printing/Advert (posters, bookmarks, social media, chapbook)	2500
Readings room rental fees	600

Staff Meetings (2) Food	215
Office supplies	200
InDesign (annual)	240
Travel (bookfair and conference—3 people)	1500
Zoom License	200
MailChimp	180
TOTAL	**5805**

Income

Department	2000
Donations	1780
Web Subscriptions @$5/annual	550
Submission Fees @$2	836
RSO Travel Fund	1000
Book Sale	720
TOTAL	**6886**

The largest expense for most undergraduate literary magazines is the printing or hosting. If your journal is online, then security software, various costs for digital management systems like MailChimp or Eventbright, social media ads, and etc.—these will be your basic "publishing" expenses, and they are sometimes not cheap. (An organization that publishes online may spend more money on in-person readings, advertising, conferences, book fairs, and travel—when possible.) Universities and colleges may also pay for some web hosting and give you web space for publishing, but this is not always the case and you may have more editorial freedom with a website that is not hosted by your institution. For print magazines, most institutions ask that you get at least three estimates from printers and they prefer that you choose the cheapest (more on this in Chapter 3, "Production"). Building a relationship with a printer is helpful as well, and can in some cases bring costs down a bit. (Appendix B lists a couple of noteworthy printers.)

As new staff comes in, the outgoing staff might need to pass along the details of various trades, costs (outstanding bills, of course), and gift/arts economy investments made in the literary community: a map, if you will, of where the organization has been, who they know, and how trades work—and any leftover business. As a new editor, be sure to ask for the outgoing

When a student journal won an award for design, other journals took notice. At conferences and festivals, the students were asked who their printer was. Not long after, the printer reported that they had gotten a lot of new work, via references from the student journal, for printing other literary journals. As a result, they were more than happy to continue working with the student editors at the award-winning journal and had a great deal of patience, moving forward with new student editors each year. (Be nice to your printers ☺.)

staff's assessment of the value they got (monetary or otherwise) from their activities. If a written list does not exist, or there are significant changes being made to the organization, you will at least have to map out a history of what has gone on (moneywise and otherwise). When proving the financial efficacy of the enterprise, the basic function is to make the "money in" match closely the "money out" for the academic year. Revenue and expenses.

A few ways to orient yourself to budgeting:

1. **Find the "money person" in your department or college or Student Activities Office.** Introduce yourself and ask about the process of moving the organization's money around—they will likely be able to tell you how things work at your institution and may therefore help you solve future problems. It's best to have a good relationship and clear path for your accounts. There may be a bank or credit union involved, connected to your student activities office. You may have to sign up as the account's "owner."

2. **Talk to the students/faculty who were involved in previous years,** if you can find them, and ask them if they can send you their budget—

At my current public institution, the student literary magazine has two accounts: one is a university "cost center" for the magazine where all the donations are stored. These donations could be from private citizens (large and small donations as a result of fundraising) as well as funding streams from the dean, the department, and other university offices and endowments. The other account is with a credit union that offers checking accounts to all the university-affiliated student organizations. Generally the former is used for printing and other "large ticket" items and the latter is used for small costs—like a dozen sandwiches for a proofreading meeting or a push notification for a Facebook event. Budgeting involves both accounts.

also ask what their greatest funding challenges were, so you are well warned. (Perhaps there is a Google Drive folder where past documents are stored.)

3. **Work with your Advisors and other editors with any questions about money**—ahead of time, so there are no unhappy surprises later and so that everyone is on the same page.

University: Student Fees, Department, College, Provost

University funding can come from a number of university entities. The ones discussed here are not put in any particular order of importance (again, every institution is different) but if you need funding and you have not tried knocking on doors yet, hopefully this section will provide a few ideas.

Student Fees

Being a registered student organization can be incredibly helpful to a student literary magazine, and it is usually not hard to become one (future editors may thank you). Registered student organizations (RSO) are a part of almost all universities, comprised of various student-led groups who meet around specific activities and represent the university's student body to the entire university community. Many of them are service oriented. There is a process for becoming a registered student group and then an annual orientation or a bit of official paperwork when new officers for the organization (your literary magazine) are put in place. As the Editor-in-Chief and staff of a student literary magazine, you sign up as "officers" and have the rights and responsibilities that come with being an RSO. (You also have to go to a few regular meetings with all the student organizations.) These groups are funded in part by student fees—those infernal extra lines of numbers on your tuition statement. Being a registered student organization gives you access to some of that money. You may also be able to get student-fee funding without being a registered student organization. Ask.

How you get that money is another thing. It may be in place, or you may have to apply and make a case for what you do: represent the university in the literary realm by publishing student writing and art, specifically student creative work. Much like a university gallery space or a theater production or a symphony, you are creating and maintaining a venue for students to practice what they are learning in the classroom in order to present it to the university community and beyond. Perhaps far beyond, in the case of student literary magazines that publish work from all over the world and (perhaps) maintain a subscription list.

Some student literary magazines only get funding from student fees if they limit the writers being published in their magazine to students attending that university. While this is understandable (check the mission statement for your registered student organization in the student activities office) you could perhaps make the case that as student editors (and to accurately reflect what you are learning about the world) you will need to invite the world into your work space and cooperate with writers from the community, the state, the region, or the world. The configuration of student fees, workspace reach, and actual funding is a constant conversation, so don't be afraid to revisit it regularly.

Student fees are usually distributed by a board or committee comprised of students, staff, faculty, even the Dean of Students. Be prepared to make your case for changes, or defend your funds, by finding out ahead how student fees are collected, processed, and distributed. (They may help you pay for a great number of things, including tuition stipends for some upper editors). You will be asked to prove how you are responsibly spending the money and fulfilling the university's mission. (How many hours do you work?) Make sure you are familiar with all the mission statements that are guiding your organization: the university's, the college's, your department's, and yours.

At a private university where the undergraduate literary magazine was a registered student organization, student fees paid a stipend for the Editor-in-Chief and three section editors—totaling about $25,000. At this private university tuition was higher than at the public university across town (still not nearly the most expensive tuition, in terms of private, nonprofit universities). The Editor-in-Chief's part of the money essentially translated to free tuition for a year. The journal had an office and a budget for "technical" costs as well. (Website, printing, equipment, etc.) At times, these staff positions were quite competitive.

Department

If your department (Humanities, English, Writing, Liberal Studies) offers writing courses—especially if they offer creative writing courses—they may be interested in showcasing what their students can do as writers and as editors. These are real world skills (writing and editing) which universities know they must teach (an effective workforce means having people who can communicate effectively). I cannot tell you the number of times I have heard business people tell me that even an English minor on an applicant's resumé catches their eye: people who study languages are seen by the business community as having the ability to write, respond, think for themselves, and parse careful meaning out of words.

By showcasing student work, I mean having a product to show to the dean, the provost, the university president—or donors, or visiting families who are interested in what students are up to at your university. In most cases it's a book, the journal printed, but a link to a web-based journal works the same way. Most departments have some ability to choose special projects they fund—despite what they may say. ("We have no control over our budget!" means they probably have no control over the big total on the last line of their budget document, but all departments are given some discretionary funds for events and activities and can move funds around at least a little bit from column to column.) Again, look at your department's mission statement, course offerings, and faculty (if you have creative writing faculty, enlist their help in your cause)—these can help you shape a good argument for some funds for a specific activity (printing or web hosting or a launch party), at the very least.

College

An academic dean has to work between the university administration and the people (in departments) who attend to the courses and degree programs (students and faculty). A dean is a professor too, who serves at the behest of the college president (and can be fired as a dean) but also may be tenured faculty (and may come from or return to a "home department"). There are, likely, a number of departments under the watchful eye of the dean. (A college of the arts may include an art department, music, dance, theater, etc.) In other words, being a dean is a balancing act and a hard job. Deans get asked to support all kinds of things—conferences, new faculty lines, university initiatives to name just a few—so why not ask the dean to help fund your literary journal?

By now, you know what I am going to say: ask around about the dean (what is she like?) and look for the college's mission statement so you know what the guiding principle is for that college and that dean. Take some copies of your journal (or a bookmark with the web address) to show the dean (actually, take these to everyone at the university—put a face with the words on a page). Make an appointment and bring your planning document (your ideas spelled out plus your budget). Don't be afraid to be specific and don't be afraid to ask for more than what you absolutely need to survive. Think creatively and think big—and be prepared to back up your claims.

There are many deans and offices at the university that are not considered academic—a Dean of Students, for instance. There are Residential Life Offices, and Admissions Offices. Take the Admissions Office, for instance. They might be especially interested in your literary magazine. The journal is proof of student life and the array of skills that courses support—plus it is run by students and is creative and probably kind of fun. Remember that some funding (or trade) may come from these other offices partnering with you in presenting an activity, for instance a reading. You bring the writers, and they bring the snacks or provide a wonderful venue. Don't forget to consider these non-academic entities in your planning.

Provost

The Provost is the chief academic officer at your institution and may also (like a dean) be a tenured faculty member who might come from or return to an academic department. They no doubt, just like a dean, have a department affiliation—in other words, a background in teaching, research, and service. Read the university's website about the current Provost.

Provosts don't often have a lot to do directly with students day to day, but are more likely to meet with and be focused on faculty. This is not to say they are not interested in students—indeed they are and should be. After all, they are overseeing the part of the university (the academic side) where students do their work and earn degrees. While they stand between the academic colleges and the university president, they also want to showcase the hard work and genius of the students. Because this is the most powerful person on the academic side, your mouth may be a little drier while talking to the Provost. It may be harder to get an appointment. And while you may wonder if you should tell your dean and department chair that you are going to the Provost for funds, you should not shy away from asking the Provost for funds. You might even ask your advisor, chair, and/or dean to come along and help support your effort.

It's true that most requests for funds start with student organizations and work their way up to the Provost, but you can also ask for different things from each of these entities. For instance, perhaps you would like to run a writing contest (fiction, poetry, nonfiction—the usual) and you need some money for an award. A Provost might be particularly interested in that, since it would support the idea that the provost's office is directly connected to student success. You could show them exactly how you would run the contest from start to finish, with a carefully built timeline. (Try including all registered students from all university departments—there may be a fantastic writer who is not sitting next to you in Fiction Forms; the Provost is there

As editors of literary journals, we can't assume university administrators, staff, faculty, and students will understand what we do. It can be frustrating to describe the value over and over again, but it's worthwhile; development offices are key to finding potential donors, and administrative support makes funding and events much easier. Always be sure your university's development office and president's office, and your college's dean's office, receive at least one free copy. Ask the development office if they'd like more copies to provide alums or possible donors.

—Abigail Cloud, Faculty Advisor, *Prairie Margins*,
Bowling Green State University

to support those students too.) The winners could be published in your journal, even. Perhaps some of the Provost's money could go for awards, and another portion could go toward publishing costs. Of course there may be other things you could ask for—start with your highest priority if the Provost is your last stop.

Advisory Board

A "board" can be many different things, and I'm bringing up an "advisory board" here as a subcategory because it is probably the easiest thing to put together for your undergraduate literary magazine. An advisory board is a group of people who advise—there is no expectation that they will raise money (unless you make it clear that you expect them to) but there is the expectation that they will do the work to understand the organization and they will be engaged in certain activities to a limited extent. They are there to support you, not interfere. Advisory boards typically help connect the organization to the community, engage in "steering committee" activities (they might help decide the next editor, for instance, or help the editor sort through applications and interview section editors), and attend or help organize events. With any board, you need to spell out, clearly, what you expect board members to do. If you already have a board, be sure to read their by-laws so you know how they have been instructed to intersect with what you do. You can also draw up by-laws if you are creating an advisory board. (Google "non-profit arts organization by-laws" and you will get lots of examples to choose from.)

You might opt for a "board of directors"—this is typically a board with more power to drive the organization as well as bring in money. They can donate themselves or bring other donors in. These are more typical of stand-alone nonprofits.

The advisory board I worked with at *Glass Mountain* changed over the years, but one thing has not: in a pinch, the board members show up. The first board chair I worked with did a fabulous job of helping with fundraising and talking me off the ledge when the funding questions got sticky at the college level. She also put together the board's by-laws. The second board chair helped with diversifying the board and got the board more involved with the annual conference for new writers, Boldface. When new staff choices got to be really tough, over the summer, a few board members stepped in to review the application materials and make their own recommendations. In another instance, two board members stepped up to join a third who had funded a student-poet scholarship to the annual summer writing conference.

When putting together a board, think about the community surrounding the university: the artists, the business people, the professionals. You will no doubt find people who care about the arts, and care about writing, visual arts, and performing arts. Think in terms of diversity, getting a variety of people involved. It is good to have the board members cycle on and off in a regular pattern, and to have a schedule of monthly or semiannual meetings ahead of time (it can be very hard to get even a small group of people with full lives to agree on a meeting time). It is always good to have an open conversation between the board and your upper editors to make sure that everyone has an idea of each other's interests, approaches to ideas, and personalities. Working with a board can help you form future professional connections. It's also a great exercise in "assume nothing and ask lots of questions." Your board members probably have a wealth of experience that you can depend on.

Fundraising 101

No matter what your budget or the promise of funds from one or another of the entities listed above (or others—there are a lot of ways to go about this) you may have to go look for funding for something specific that you want to do. Warning: raising money is a state of mind. You have to be enthusiastic about the project. You have to be ready to answer questions. What are you raising money for? Who is going to benefit from this? How is a donor going to know that their contribution has made an impact? (Why is your project necessary? How is it helpful? The ways of phrasing your intent are numerous and the particular view that your specific donors will have is worth considering.) Next to being prepared, you also have to come off as committed and certain. You have to make sure that what you say is

One of our on-campus fundraising activities is to collect book donations and wrap them in brown paper to be sold as "Blind Date with a Book." Months later, we hold a Book Swap, which helps build literary community.
—Catherine Zobal Dent, Faculty Advisor of *RiverCraft* and FUSE, Susquehanna University

going to happen, will actually happen—web events, printing, a co-sponsored reading, an invitation to a writer or editor you'd like your staff to meet, a jointly sponsored one-day conference on editing/revising. You probably need to organize your whole group toward the task of selling yourselves. Fundraising events, which happen over a given time (a month, a week, a day), are how you typically raise money. Fundraisers (people) are good at asking for things. Primarily money, yes, but other things too. Co-sponsoring, by the way, is mentioned here because it could be considered a form of fundraising: working with another (maybe literary) group to pool resources and come up with a plan that would help you create value for participants. If you are approaching anyone for help, you have to do some basic things to prepare.

To begin, put together some materials that describe your organization. Make a list of recent events/publications/activities and future actions you hope to host. Take a look at the people your journal has published in the past—what did they go on to do? How many submissions have you had or do you hope to have for the next issue? Who are the organizations you have partnered with, or hope to partner with? If you have some photos of past events or can put together a short video that describes what you do and shows students engaged in the work .... You get the idea. Collect these materials and have them ready.

Some people take to fundraising and others (for example me) hate to actually *ask* people they know for a monetary contribution. Here are a few things to know:

1. A request for money is called an "ask"
2. Universities and colleges all have an office that deals with asking for money—called the "funding office" or "development" (something less obvious than "philanthropy"); find that office and ask if there is a process or policy for students requesting donations for specific projects (and don't let them tell you that students cannot do that—it happens with sports teams, university scholarships, your university art gallery, on and on)
3. Find out what you need to do to get a dedicated account at the university where the cash donations can be kept; donations that go through the university and are tagged for your organization should be tax

deductible, which will help your donors be confident that the money will be properly taken care of as well as giving the donor a nice deductible to include in their tax filing next year

4. Ask how the money you may raise will be handled by the university—make sure you get everything you raise, not merely a cut

5. Avoid asking for money from someone (a person, an organization or a foundation) that you know gives money to another organization on campus that is similar to yours—at least not without asking that sister-organization if it's okay to ask (people get VERY protective of their funding sources, for good reason, obviously)

6. Before you ask anyone, get to know the donor's possible interest in what you do *and* what/who they might already be giving money to that would complement (or contradict) this gift

7. You can always do a bake sale, a dinner, a raffle, or a silent auction event but those will probably not bring in a large chunk of money, though they might raise your profile and let people know that you exist, which can lead to larger cash donations; you can even practice "asking" when the staff gets to socialize with donors who are interested in what you are doing (because they show up!); bottom line, find your inner party planner.

Fundraising takes time and preparation. I'm not saying this to discourage you. It is easy to plan a little bit each week until you have something to launch—like a crowd-funding campaign. But you might need some facts and figures, some evidence. (It is not always easy to come up with action photos of people reading and writing or sitting and listening to someone who has their face

At one point, our development office decided to work with a crowdfunding startup that focused on raising money for small academic projects—like uniforms for a crew team, travel for Middle-Eastern studies classes, and our literary conference. The crowd-funding startup was—we quickly learned—barely just starting. It was rough going (when we found they hadn't really connected everything up) but we had the assistance of a person on the university's development team. We put together text and images to explain what we were doing and why, who was involved and how—lots of info plus a three-minute video edited by a very generous person in the communications department (we filmed about fifteen interviews on an iPad and sent the raw footage). We sent out hundreds of emails over a month's time, to scores of targeted lists that we comprised from old email lists (with plenty of time spent updating). We raised about 7.5K—not our goal of 10K, but we did raise the last 2.5K the old-fashioned way, by calling people up and asking for a contribution.

in a (note)book, but what about a group shot of your editors meeting to discuss submissions? The crowd at a reading? A video of a reader delivering an impressive short poem?) Short clips can simply be comprised of student editors talking about what they are learning from working at the magazine. Get an Instagram story started. Or three. Post links to other social media accounts who follow yours. Again, if questions arise about what you are asking for and why, you need to know how money moves through the financial accounts available to you, through your organization, and you probably need permission from your advisor and department to put out, publicly, the fundraising materials you compose. Ask questions and don't be deterred.

It is fair to ask your development office if they could work with you on fundraising, but the answer may be that it will take years to see any result. Think hard about this. Do you have the patience to move a project forward without seeing the benefit in the time you have at the university? Are you willing to spend a little time moving the project forward by increments so that someone in your position, in the future, gets what they need? The answer could be yes (or no), but be sure to discuss this with your staff, advisors, and department chair before choosing a path for or against that worthy effort of paying it forward.

And don't forget to thank your donors. Whether the university sends thank you notes or not, it's a good idea for you to do so. Keep names and addresses and phone numbers—and keep them for your use only (privacy!). A short note, handwritten by a student editor, can mean that the donor remembers you the next time.

Faculty Advisor/Graduate Advisor

Most official student groups have a faculty advisor, most likely someone whose area of expertise lies in the area of the group's interest. For you, this would probably be a writer on the faculty who has also been an editor. You may very well find a willing faculty member in your creative writing program, or in the Humanities, Liberal Arts, Languages or Writing departments. Depending on how your journal and academic unit are configured, that person could be more or less involved in the day-to-day matters of running your literary journal. Some faculty advisors check in a couple of times of semester, others are charged by their departments to meet weekly with the student editors and are given a list of things that have to get done. And then there's the vast space in between. The bottom line here, as always, is to be very clear from the outset, if possible, concerning what the advisors' duties entail.

You might be surprised how many of your department faculty have had previous experience with student publications—maybe when they themselves were students. Perhaps they were interns at a press or periodical—for class credit or tuition stipends or simply for fun while they were starting their

As a faculty advisor, I have spent many evenings and weekends (at proofing meetings for instance) listening to undergraduates argue the relative merits of specific Toni Morrison novels—and impress me with their level of knowledge on language and literature (including grammar!). When I hear colleagues bemoan the disinterest or carelessness of their students, I remark on how lucky I am to work with the best word-nerds ever: student editors. If you are a writer/teacher, and you really do care about words on a page or spoken from a stage with eloquence, consider being a faculty advisor for a student literary magazine. It is incredibly rewarding.

careers. Graduate students, too, can be advisors. They too work as editors—at university journals, during the break between semesters, or doing a little private editing for money (helping someone write a book or article), if not in an official university assistantship at a professional journal. Most academics write and edit their own work and sometimes the work of colleagues—so they know their way around a manuscript. You might have to ask around a bit—or even have a ready list of questions for potential advisors. Make sure you have the same vision of the job. If there is a lot of interest, conduct interviews (ask your department chair about this). No matter what, you want to emphasize good communication with your advisor by setting up a clear set of guidelines on who is responsible for what. You want everyone to agree (as much as possible) on what will happen going forward.

As a faculty advisor I am prone to extol the virtues of being a faculty advisor: engaged, detail-oriented, helpful, guiding, encouraging, knowledgeable about the university as well as small press publishing, and with a sense of when to back off and let the students (or any particular student, according to her/his/their skills) do the work. It's not a job for the average research-oriented faculty member, but it can be depending on the university resources, on department policies, and on the students in charge of the journal. (In other words, advising a journal can be a nice break from the work of single-minded research or committee work.) It is very rewarding, sometimes frustrating, and almost always frenetic since the students are also students and have a lot of work to do elsewhere—if not jobs and families who need their attention too. Flexibility and an even temper will help when being an advisor. Familiarity with university offices and structures is a must. A little bit of knowledge concerning what therapists in private practice do might also help.

From the student perspective, it is best to choose someone who is known for follow-through and commitment, a tenured faculty member (who has fewer people ahead in the university hierarchy to please on the day-to-day), a creative writing faculty member if possible (who understands the writer's side), and someone who has good connections to other university entities (the department, the college, the library and bookstore, the development office, etc.). All these things are rarely possible in one person (you might be interested in a pair of co-advisors), but preparing your questions and asking around is a good idea. Remember, no tenured faculty member is required to do anything like this—so don't approach anyone as if you are doing them a favor. (If they get a course release for the advising position, that is a much better situation. Such arrangements aren't too common but you might be able to help them make a case for it.) You will often be directed toward tenure-track faculty—people who are earning their membership card in the academy and have not gone through the tenure process yet. Be careful here, as the workload of a tenure-track faculty member often includes publishing (writing a book, let's say) as a bottom line with a time limit. They may be stretched with the array of service commitments they must satisfy in time for a tenure review. You need someone who is interested, *reasonably available*, and can offer some institutional guidance.

If your journal is also an RSO, you will have to have a faculty advisor—most registered student organizations require one, and some affiliated financial institutions (as mentioned, a bank or credit union that works with your RSO office to provide checking accounts to student groups) may require the faculty advisor to be a signatory on that account. Some faculty may balk at that fiduciary responsibility, but clear policies on the access and use of the money should forestall any … errors. Some faculty, through the Human Resources Department, carry academic insurance policies in case anything goes wrong in the course of their duties as faculty, which it rarely does, but the insurance can be helpful as backup.

I can't think of a case where funds were used improperly, though I have kept close track of the bank accounts (the ID/Passwords and charges logged) when I've been a faculty advisor. I do know of faculty members who have had to use that academic insurance for other matters related to their work as faculty—so the best is a multipurpose academic insurance policy. Remember, students typically involve themselves in student literary organizations to learn about publishing and the business of writing, not because there are a lot of resources lying around or because it is risky business.

If you have a handbook for your literary journal—a policy and procedures manual that spells out everyone's job and makes the mission and activities clear (see Chapters 3 and 4)—that would help in getting a faculty member or a graduate advisor involved. A graduate advisor—a graduate student who serves a similar function as the faculty advisor—could be very helpful, especially if that person has a teaching assistantship which allows them to "teach" one of their required undergraduate classes as an advisor to a literary journal. Graduate advisors often have a unique view from their positions as not-quite-only students and not-quite-faculty. They are often teaching courses and taking courses too. Again, the duties must also be clearly spelled out in a document that everyone can reference, even if

As the graduate advisor, I found my role was primarily divided between organization and communication. Our program had a semester-length class, a practicum, devoted to the management and curation of a literary magazine. I dealt with what student editors were discussing: their likes, dislikes, and boundaries. Along with them, I'd hash out the details of a task on a classroom white board. (I'm a very visual person and I find charting, grouping, color-coding immensely helpful with the practical side.) We identified what decisions had to be made and how we would move forward. We also devoted time to the theories behind our decisions. The assigned essays helped us to be better equipped to make informed decisions when the time came. But if you are strapped for time, which we often were, the theoretical can be the first thing to fall away. However, I must say that keeping up on the theoretical study created a remarkable shorthand for student communication. Josephine Mitchell, MFA.
    —Graduate Advisor, *Glass Mountain Magazine*, 2017–2018

it's not in the student literary journal's handbook. If you can get both, the faculty advisor would be well served to have a graduate advisor/assistant to work with. An institution that has both (like University of Houston) is putting a lot of investment in student learning while also recognizing the value of faculty involvement outside of traditional coursework. There might be required weekly meetings with students, or regular reporting to a chair or division, but that keeps things on track. It is possible that a graduate student in creative writing (if you have a creative writing MFA or PhD program at your university—or even an MA in English or Liberal Studies, let's say) would be able to offer their career interest as newbies to the professional publishing realm. (In other words, they may know a lot about publishing in literary journals.) If your institution has professional journals or a university press (see below) which includes literary publishing, they are probably staffed at least in part by graduate students. Graduate students working with undergraduates and faculty, all together, is a dream—and perhaps the shape of higher ed to come (see Chapter 5).

Partner Journals and University Presses

If there are other professional journals in your area—either campus-affiliated (perhaps at your university press or a scholarly journal in your department or another humanities department) or in the local community—you might consider contacting them and asking for a tour (after you've thoroughly combed their website). Take a look at what they are doing, how they function and what their financial situation is. Don't be afraid to approach them and ask if they can explain how they operate financially or how they manage tasks—they can always say no if it's an inconvenience. But if they say *Yes* you might get some very useful information. They are probably nonprofits, like you, and have to function, at least in part, on the kindness of strangers. BTW, don't be stealing their strangers (see above, on fundraising.) Remember to be a good neighbor to other publishing and literary organizations and respect what they do. Find a way to compliment each other, not repeat what each other does or compete for limited resources.

There might be opportunities to co-sponsor events with local or university publishers: readings, book fairs, literary festivals, or even professionalization activities. You could come together, with the help of your graduate advisor, and run a workshop for students and community writers on submitting creative work to journals, agents, and publishers. You might co-sponsor a slam poetry event or a workshop on how to handle being a writer on a stage with a mic in your face. How about local veteran writers or LBGTQ+ writers, a Writers-in-the-Schools organization, or a LatinX writers group? You probably have a wide range of people taking writing classes at your university or college. Ask them if they might be interested in a literary event that addresses issues of mental health, (dis)abilities, or identity. As a nexus of literary wonderments and as a willing partner organization, be open and welcoming to a range of activities that serve all the writers around you.

A partner journal or university press might also offer internships—for course credit or a small stipend. (Ask a department advisor about how internships work in your department.) Your journal's staff could earn credit and learn how another, perhaps larger, literary organization or publisher operates day to day from firsthand experience—and get some ideas on to handle your organization's challenges (more on internships in Chapter 6).

Your advisors, faculty, department chair, or college office might be able to help you put together a list of local or state-wide literary and/or arts organizations. And don't be surprised if your university has a number of offices engaged in publishing, whether they are combined under the umbrella of a university press or they are separate, housed in various colleges and departments and covering a wide array of professional concerns. Most universities have, at the very least, an alumni magazine. In fact, the Alumni Office might be particularly interested in your publishing activities. After all, your former editors are alum.

University presses are also, of course, stretched for resources and many of them focus on only a few types of books or journals—perhaps history texts or a social science journal. Every university press is different and they are all rather complicated, meaning it might take some explaining re: how they operate. (Any time you start asking questions and someone is willing to explain, thank them profusely—it is a gift of their time.) It is almost a surety that many people have put decades of work into putting together a university press. There may have even been quite political discussions and shrinking commitments and budgets involved. What I'm trying to say is,

Local literary organizations may include a Writers-in-the-Schools group or community writing workshops housed in a local recreation center or even a small publishing group running writer residencies. Larger cities are, of course, more likely to have plenty of literary groups, but small towns have local writers too. Writing is a lonesome activity, so while you can't always tell how much time a writer (or editor) might want to spend working on an event or activity with other people, you can probably count on the fact that general interest in the literary arts is there somewhere in your geographical area. A book club may have members who enjoy a poetry reading now and again. Your university will probably look very kindly on your community outreach. Think creatively to build something that has long-lasting buy-in and return interest.

don't be surprised by a slight ... chill in the air ... when you approach a university press with questions about their structure or financials. It isn't about you—but is probably about time and money and effort that has been stretched and stretching for years and years.

⭑Advertising ⭒

You have to get the word out about your submission period, your new issues, and your events. Posters, social media, email, lawn signs? The obvious answer is yes, do all four and more. You will have to design an ad campaign for the exact event, audience, and situation. (And no yard signs during a snowstorm or hurricane, right?) If the event is off campus, make sure the ads include the address, the date, the time. How obvious, the details, right? Try creating a checklist. (For months, a magazine in our area had a letter missing in the title at the top of their homepage—it took a new staff member, eight months after the page's redesign, to notice the misspelling. It happens.)

These ad materials (and the designing) require money and attention. Editing the materials can take more than one set of eyes, of course, but first you must build and confirm an advertising strategy. You will need a system to figure out what is needed, what it will cost, and what you hope to get in return. In a very helpful scenario, one of your editors is getting a minor in marketing. Or your social media editor is also involved in Greek Life and has some effective ideas she's used to reach interested parties in the past. Your staff should amplify whatever social media posts you put up. Everyone needs to get involved in advertising these days, spreading the word. Make sure you have a Facebook, Twitter, and Instagram account—at least (see "Social Media" below).

Remember that your faculty and other students won't show up if they don't know about your event, your sale, your submission deadline. Having a PR person on staff, whether or not you have a social media editor, is basic.

If your university has a business school, you might advertise there first for a Public Relations person, someone to generate ad copy, work with your design team to create the graphics, and keep track of the various strategies you use to advertise. (You have to keep track of what you send out: old, leftover posts and posters, stagnant web pages, schedules changed and not updated ... they all signal to your audience that you aren't fully paying attention and they might not bother to check back again.) Fundraising events, submission deadlines, calls for new editors, announcements on readings and other events, award notices—they all require advertising strategies that include reminders and updates. And you are all writers, yes? So you might have to help write the ad copy, postings, or emails. Your art editor might have to produce some graphics when your design person is busy—or you might have a dedicated graphics editor. You might visit the front-office person at the Art Department (Communications Department or University Communications and Outreach) for help with your requests for an email blast to their faculty and students. (You can also do this through contacts you've made with students and faculty in other departments.) All of this takes coordination but is 100 percent worth the bother when you get donations, your submissions grow, and/or your events are well attended.

Once you create advertising materials, archive the files. Google Drive is one storage venue, but your university or college might have their own server where you have access to storage (make hard-drive backups of everything too—you can never be too careful with digital work). These files are potential templates for those who join the organization after you leave. I cannot stress enough how useful these archives can be. Once someone has gone to the trouble to create a form or a system or even a really good excel page or email message, why not store it and save someone else's valuable time when that part of the year comes around again? They can revise, update, adjust, reconfigure—and they will be thrilled that they don't have to start from scratch.

One of the most common errors I've seen in advertising for student literary events, journals, and outreach is material produced without enough information. Double check, triple check, that all the relevant info is there (including icons for Instagram, Facebook, Twitter—whatever your online presence entails). Make sure the Facebook Event, for instance, has all the correct info—who is the featured reader, when and where the event is, how they can find your web page, maybe a map, and always include contact info for questions. Lately the general design style has been for more minimalist postings and pages, and that's fine, that's great, as long as all the relevant info is featured in a readable and pleasing way. Don't put the date on the poster in a ten-point font and expect that people will know when your event is; don't hide the info about the event that people will normally be looking

The most common complaint I've heard from student editors is that no one at the university or college knows about the literary magazine. People they talk to haven't come across it, and maybe don't even know what a literary magazine is. The students, the faculty, and the staff at your college or university are your first market. Remember that advertising for student literary magazines is probably less about sales and more about exposure, about finding the people (students and community writers) who might be interested no matter what their career hopes or professional background. People who like to read or who know the university might read your literary magazine or even submit their own work—or tell someone else about the opportunities offered for new writers. Whether your magazine is university-based, local, regional or statewide, national or international, people at the university are always your audience because they want to know what is going on in the hallowed halls. Look around at how other university entities advertise themselves to the university community—and make a plan to get some attention. Digital signboards in common areas? Find the office that administrates content.

for at the bottom of your home page; put the info needed *now* at the top. No one wants to spend time trying to find information that should be obvious. And try something to get attention, yes. Try new typefaces, wild colors, weird images, but don't frustrate people. Help them find you.

Class Visits

Another way to reach students who might be nearby and yet uninformed (so much email, so little time) is through class visits. These can happen face-to-face or online. At a smaller institution your staff might be able to visit every class in your home department. Divide and conquer. Remember to visit a few art/design/businesses/music/dance/theater classes, too, during the first couple of weeks of the academic year, term, or semester. At larger institutions, you can probably at least cover the creative writing courses. Make sure every one of your staff persons who is conducting a class visit has a script they can access on their phone (or print it out), plus a copy of the journal to pass around (or take a small stack of bookmarks with the web address). That staff person should be correctly informed enough to do a confident and reasonable job of speaking about the journal and answering questions. To help out, create a handout to distribute (on paper or digitally) with all the relevant dates of events and deadlines coming up plus an email address for inquiries.

Find the instructors of the courses you'd like to visit, first, of course, through a very politely worded email request with all the details of what you are asking for (attention for a submission deadline, an upcoming reading, etc.) and an assurance that you won't go over ten minutes (leaving time in there for questions from the students). And once the instructor says yes, be sure to send a reminder (and ask for confirmation of the location and time) the day before your visit. Done early and well, class visits might also help you connect with students who might apply for staff positions. Take a few copies of a staff application form—or, again, distribute something with the web info. Perhaps ask them to fill it out and return it right then—or send it to the editor's email address ASAP.

Email Lists

Of course you are going to collect email addresses at events, book fairs, and really at any opportunity, right? Put your managing editor in charge of this one, or your PR person. Input those addresses right away to your email-handling platform. MailChimp is one of those—remember that they require you *only* email people who have agreed to receive emails from your organization. (And if people ask to be removed, take them off right away.) MailChimp plays fair and has, like a lot of web-based communication platforms, a free (or cheap) function and then several membership levels you can purchase.

You can also create your own email lists and store them in a spread sheet for easy use. Community list, submission list, staff-of-yesteryear lists, and more—keep them all, each for their own specific use. In addition, your home department probably has the ability to send out your emails to students, faculty, and staff (don't keep those email lists—let the department maintain those active lists because they constantly change). Get to know the person in the department's front office who sends out department emails and make sure they are your friend. They might be the person who does room reservations, too—that person is your very best friend; and remember, always treat staff—regardless of what they do—with utmost respect. They are the people that make everything possible for everyone at your college or university, and it is not in their job description to get thanked. However, it is in your job description to thank the people who help you.

Notice the term "email lists"—you will not have one list, you will have many. For staff applications, for instance, you are only sending the announcement to students at the institution (and maybe only in your college or department, it depends). For event announcements like readings and open mics you may want to include faculty who could either attend or remind their students (many creative writing faculty ask that their students attend a reading and report back to them or the class about the event). Is your reading in a restaurant or pub and are you having an open mic after? Send that announcement to your community list. If you are sending out a request for donations, include the former staff list, your former donor list, an alumni list if you know someone with access to that, plus almost all your other lists. Recall that in some cases you might have to adjust the salutation to fit the list—and even some of the other language in your email will have to be edited appropriately. This really matters: no one is going to keep reading an email that is clearly not addressed to them. In fact, always have at least one other set of eyes go over your email before you send—proofreading is especially important in your case because you are, yes, editors.

Here's another thing about email management: you MUST have email lists with clear parameters and you must maintain them. That means adding people and taking them off, scrubbing for duplicates and checking for spelling errors when emails come back "undeliverable." Regular (at least twice a semester) maintenance can be boring and methodical, but sometimes that kind of close attention is a good place to sit for a while—it's a quiet activity. With email lists that are properly maintained, your decisions and actions (effective communication) can be so much more smooth and easy. No one wants to start a new action with a broken wheel. Also, keep a detailed log of what's gone out and to whom. File a copy of the email in your archives—as mentioned, it might be a good template for another time. This record-keeping matters. When someone brings up the fact that—oops!—you need to send out a reminder for that reading tomorrow night, the log will let you know if someone already sent that out.

Social Media

Social media is curating some of our biggest conversations. Using social media to the advantage of your journal is rather simple: you simply have to

University Archives exist in the university library to store the work that the university has done over the years. Get in touch with your archive librarian and find out if they already have an archive for your magazine, if your magazine has been around a while. Perhaps they want to start one if they don't already have one. This is a gift to posterity. (You can tell potential donors about it, too.) Your journal may go on for decades. One day there might be a celebration at your university that focuses on publications—and your work could be featured. An archive would include one or two copies of each issue of the magazine, but it might also have a few posters, fliers, photos—whatever you've produced that looks really impressive and lets people in the future know what you were up to and who helped out. I've seen students get the housekeeping bug and throw out boxes of old material just because they were old—don't do that unless you absolutely have to. Publication offices always have boxes and boxes of books and posters and journals around. Hold on. Be a good archivist and honor the work of those before you: call the library.

post informative and interesting content and then figure out how to amplify those posts—creating traffic toward your website, submission manager, events, or journal orders. The point is to present your active face. Hit the right pitch: what varieties of material, how many posts, revisited how often? You probably have many people on staff who can contribute content—students always say they can. But again, you need a plan, a strategy—and probably a graphics person. Advertising for submissions, posting event information, sharing moments from events, keeping in touch with your writers and readers, and making a good story (Instagram, TikTok) about what the organization does all day—this needs to be produced, curated, and maintained.

It might be time to state the obvious: writers are not exactly an image-producing demographic. We read and write—sit at desks and in chairs with our chins down staring at words. How many images can you produce of pens, hands, keyboards, stacked books, texts, etc. During your events, you might get photos of people standing at mics (a slam event can provide some excellent action photos) or groups of people facing one direction paying attention, maybe capturing the ambience of the venue. Whatever you choose for social media, you need someone to produce the images, correctly process the photos for the platform and contact (whenever necessary) the people in the photos for permission. Your editorial staff, hopefully, can offer images of smiling faces and busy meeting places. But a graphics person can do colorful, expressionistic work and use other images (again, be aware of permissions) that represent the vibe or brand. If you have a general set of colors, your logo, some standard format—even if it changes a bit annually to reflect the new crew—you can also signal quickly to viewers "It's us! Your favorite Undergrad Lit Mag!"

A social media editor is a good idea, someone to create the plan and present it to the group. (Also, it's best, though not always possible, if at least two pairs of eyes go over any content before it's posted.) The basic point is to highlight the work of your journal: You are promoting the creative work of artists and writers and perhaps musicians. You can link to your contributing writers' social media too, amplify their posts. Think how encouraging it is to post a photo of the upcoming cover art or a new writer reading on stage (maybe for the first time). People who were at the event, the writers themselves, the friends who couldn't make it—they will all know the journal is paying attention to promoting the work of others—and that will bring people back. Of course, while it is very easy to publicly acknowledge people, always ask before you post a recognizable image of anyone. At minimum, get their approval via email.

You are probably signing up for all the usual platforms: Instagram, Facebook, Twitter, and maybe TikTok or others. None of these are nice—

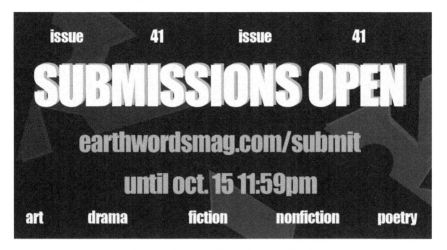

issue   41   issue   41

SUBMISSIONS OPEN

earthwordsmag.com/submit

until oct. 15 11:59pm

art   drama   fiction   nonfiction   poetry

FIGURE 2.1 *An event banner from* earthwords'*s Facebook page.*

they collect our data and use us as much or more as we use them, yes. Right now, however, your literary organization is expected to have these in place. People will go there to get an idea of who you are and what you do. (If you want to look active, your social media presence has to be active: old and out-of-date posts can make it look like you don't care.) When you sign up for these platforms, have the organization sign up for the official accounts—and use the official organizational email address(es) for editors. Have a place to store passwords so that only the right people can find them (the social media editor or person responsible). Avoid having people sign up for accounts using their personal email—they might be gone next year, leaving the organization unable to access their own accounts. People who initiate and plan to use social media platforms for the group should be the people who have been around long enough to be certifiably dependable, and creative (a bit of a graphics background will always help), with a good amount of reasonable judgment. And remember, the posts should align with the journal as a whole, so ask yourselves, before you post, if what you are doing serves the organization and its brand. The graphics have to be visually appealing and contain the correct info, of course, but also reflect the journal's aesthetic whenever and however possible.

And don't forget humor—a well-placed meme does wonders.

Then you have to figure out which platform to assign the post and when to launch it, exactly. A social media editor will be someone who already (probably) has experience with these entities themselves and knows what it takes to effectively use the individual platforms. So Twitter is one place to post your event announcement—with Facebook, however, you can create a banner that shouts the basic info, easily visible for someone who is quickly planning their day (see Figure 2.1). Twitter might be a place where you support other organizations (retweet their best stuff, amplify a post about the writer who read at your event last month, etc. See Figure 2.2) or to post quick video and/or include links to your website with pithy statements about something new that's featured there. Facebook Events is great for

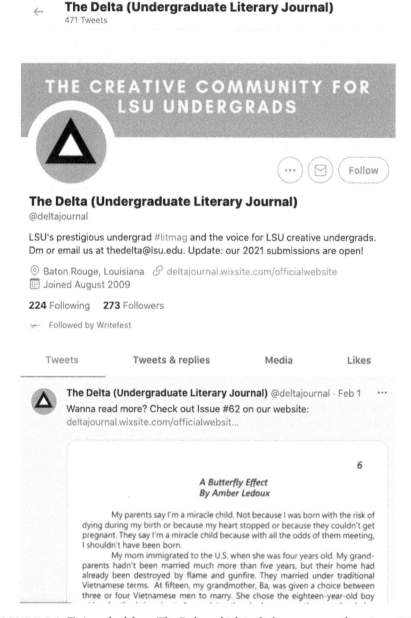

FIGURE 2.2 *Twitter feed from* The Delta *which includes an excerpt from Issue #62.*

your big moments, and Facebook Live might be appropriate for streaming an event that you'd like to spread far and wide. Instagram? Put that great poster or flier up there—or try Instagram Stories leading up to an event to highlight the fun and use it afterward to let people know that you had a crowd and things happened. If you have a virtual reading (Eventbright might work for handling registrations, if you want a little more control), post the announcement everywhere with clear directions on where to find (or sign up for) the meeting link. And keep that info front and center on social media the day before and day of the event.

Using hashtags effectively is another piece of the social media puzzle. Find and utilize hashtags that connect with the specific content you are posting. All you need is a Twitter account to get a good general idea of which hashtags are functioning for your purpose. (Remember, subject matter counts: if someone finds your magazine because you included some photos of classic cars and tweeted #classiccars, and they love the other art and stories they find on your website, success!) For instance, if you are posting a short poem about street art, you might include #streetart or #urbanart. If you are in a medium-sized city, try #literary[name of city] for your next reading. Look through your magazine's latest issue and make a list of the likely hashtags. Use a few for each posting you do that mentions the new issue—spread them out over time.

Social media trends also change quickly. It's highly likely that a lot of what I say here will have shifted by the time this book is printed and in your hands. Is TikTok going to stay in the mix? There may be new posting rules. When will Instagram be eclipsed by the next sensation? Just know this: a dedicated social media person on staff (or at least a social media plan for all to follow) can help the whole organization get the right kind of attention. Remember, too, that much of your social media will point to your organization's website: you need to know your way around the organization's staff and website so the correct info and links end up in posts (and on the website pages). You have to be able to point someone with an inquiry in the right direction, easily, so you don't lose their attention. While your staff may assure each other, right now, that they will know what to do with social media, you need an organizer—someone with some real social media savvy. Make a schedule of posting dates. (I know I'm repeating myself.) This is especially important if you plan on putting a lot of work into any new initiatives. Your audience needs to know—and be reminded so they keep checking back for more literary treasures. Post some short poems or flash fiction gems so people can understand your aesthetic.

Start by inviting a discussion with staff on the use of social media, get some feedback, check in regularly on what you are doing, and never post something mean or simply wrong. Keep everything direct, clear, correct, and inviting.

Other communication platforms mentioned here and discussed in upcoming chapters could be useful to the organization's activities. Check the Bloomsbury Academic site for this book, and specifically Appendix B, included here, for more suggestions on all kinds of digital resources. Right now, Google Drive is a dependable place to store your files. Teams works well for inter-office communication (your school might have a Microsoft 365 license). Gmail accounts (very easy to set up) can be convenient for basic communication functions plus a Google calendar that everyone can access from anywhere. Please check—you may already have an email account, a Gmail address, or your college or university might have assigned an email account or your RSO membership might come with one. Whatever you do, make sure you are not going against a school policy. (You might be able to get digital storage or an email manager through the university too. Be sure you understand the basics of the school's software user policies.) For intraoffice communication, GroupMe is popular right now and works well for quick messaging to targeted groups in your organization. Slack is a wonderful office communication tool for keeping your organization informed and for continuing conversations, plus it intersects well with Google Drive. More of these helpful digital platforms are listed in Appendix B.

Inevitably there are periods when your journal will have a less active online presence—often over summer, when everyone is taking a break, a much-needed breather. Take old announcements down and let your Twitter home sit with a nice graphic or maybe the info on the next submission deadline. If you want to keep active all year, however, having some material to post over the summer (Instagram: what writing/editing activities are your new staff engaging in right now on that beautiful summer lake?) can keep your audience awake and aware. Consider blog posts on your website or Facebook page about the writing process or offer some writing prompts. Run a contest over summer—engage your social media platforms and start the fall semester with an audience. Try a new-staff slush pile reading of contest submissions for an icebreaker in August or September: new staff can read, discuss, (re)connect, and review the schedule of events for the year ahead.

3

Editing Your Journal

The exciting part of putting together a literary journal comes with finding the literary gems you want to publish—and then having your team take them through production to the final product: artfully crafted words on a page or website. Whether your submissions happen within the confines of a university or you are taking in creative works internationally (or anything in between), the happiness in finding that surprising story, poem, essay, artwork, musical composition, review/interview, or article is like nothing else. Putting the whole publication together is another sort of composing bliss (not without effort, but certainly exciting). Experiencing the group's satisfaction when several members recognize the same wonderful submission (or connection between pieces you've chosen) is a feeling beyond measure. You are on the way, together.

Along with the moments of clarity, however, there are moments that require more perspective and patience. Some of what you read—and process and publish—will not be immediately simple to handle. There will be plenty of material you can pass on pretty quickly—sure. But many otherwise wonderful pieces of writing will come to you with one, two, five (or more) fatal flaws. And some of your staff will agree and disagree on where exactly those flaws are located. Basically, while the greatest number of submissions are easily dismissed (I've never heard of a magazine where this wasn't true), and a few pieces will leap into your hands fully formed, the ones you spend the most time on are "almost there." Many new editors are surprised at the number of submissions that are not quite exact *and* not so easily dismissed. This is where being an editor gets interesting.

When working through your slush pile—all varieties of what you find there—it is a good idea to establish early on a way of speaking to each other about what you have in front of you when discussing the work of others. Go easy on the judgmental language. Be descriptive with each other about what you see. ("There seems to be an overdependence on adverbs and adjectives in this piece.") Listen to each other and don't compete to

Being Polite: Most of your communication with writers who submit to your magazine will be via email (or communication manager within submissions software). While you may or may not know the person you are communicating with, it is always best to be clear, professional (a type of language that is not natural to any of us), and concise. Nothing extra, just get to the point. You will likely need a standard rejection letter, for instance, but you may also have a slightly more encouraging version ("We hope you will consider submitting again in the future..."). But *only* use the encouraging language if you really mean it, not because you are afraid that it sounds mean or dismissive when being direct: "Thank you for submitting to ____. We regret to say that we are passing on the opportunity to publish '_____'. We appreciate that you thought of us, however, and wish you the best with your future work." The website Submittable, a popular submission manager, allows you to have a number of templates for communication with writers and artists that you can customize for specific situations (or genre sections). Always be polite. Stick to the matter at hand in a direct and fair manner and avoid getting into fussy email threads with writers who are upset or feel misunderstood.

say the most outlandish thing about someone's actual attempt to write something clever. You've probably tried to write something clever that came out sounding ultra sincere, too, yes? Everyone does. Just be aware that a professional production requires professional language—by which I mean direct, descriptive, and respectful. If everyone can do this, then everyone can count on it and you can trust each other.

Creating a Handbook with Clear Editorial Practices

Before you hit the slush pile, you might need guidelines for staff. Begin with a clear description of your organizational structure, written down and accessible to all staff members. A literary magazine handbook is essential, though it might feel like a luxury to small literary magazines just starting out or operating with a small staff on a low (or nonexistent) budget. If that's the case, start small—but do take the first step. Do what you can with what you have. Everyone always does. However. The reason for creating and maintaining a handbook is that when things get busy or stressful, a handbook can clarify processes and no one has to feel bad about it. (Whatever "it" is.) If the handbook says so (and the handbook is accessible), everyone can breathe a sigh of relief and get on with things. (See Being

Polite, above.) Handbooks are also useful when hiring. "Take a look at our handbook: this is what the job of Fiction Editor entails." So rather than thinking of a handbook as time spent on something that everyone "knows," consider it as primary to a well-functioning organization where members come and go. It's simply a guide.

All right, yes, you can't cover everything in a handbook and situations will constantly come up that could be added to the handbook or not—some situations are too esoteric to include. (You don't need a section in the handbook saying that the magazine cannot accept baby rabbits as fundraising donations.) So much happens that is complicated, or particular or rare. So it's always good to have the upper editors and your advisors consider new policies, to consider what the unintended effects of that new policy might be (new policies that address the single, rare situation). Typically, amending a functional handbook requires a plethora of diverse voices who can parse the details, pro-conning the potential changes in order to make a decent decision.

Below is a rough sample of a handbook Table of Contents that covers basic organizational elements.

Policies and Procedures (or Handbook)

[Your Literary Magazine's Name Here]

Mission Statement (you will be asked for this frequently)

_____ is a student-run literary magazine at _____ University, specializing in the publication of undergraduate writing. _____ aims to provide student editors with real-time experience spanning the publication process. _____ is intended to teach students about effective editing skills, organizational management, and consistent community outreach... [etc.] We publish work by _____ that shows an interest in the human dilemma... [etc. usually about 200 words—many examples can be found online]

Organizational Overview

- **Office** (computers, bank accounts, keys, website accounts)
- **Funding and Finance** (include account information like bank address/phone)
- **Memberships** (Is this organization a Registered Student Group, housed in Department of Languages or College X, etc., connected to a creative writing major, etc.)
- **Annual Schedule** ("A schedule of the year ahead will be completed by the upper editors by September 1ˢᵗ" etc.—see a schedule template in Appendix B)

- **Website and/or Office** (description of what needs to be maintained)
- **Diversity Statement** (description of the organization's commitment)

Staff

- **Eligibility Guidelines and Recruitment**—See Appendix B for application form
- **Meetings**—who is required at what meetings
- **Sections and Job Descriptions**
  - **Editor-in-Chief** (responsible for x, in charge of y, must z)
  - **Managing Editor** (responsible for organizational maintenance, in charge of communication, final copy, etc.)
  - **Prose Editor** (or Fiction Editor and/or NonFiction Editor— organizes reading staff, processes submissions, edits publishing choices, proofreading, etc.)
  - **Poetry Editor** (same)
  - **Art Editor** (solicits submissions from art department, local artists, processes submissions, designs x and y, etc.)
  - **Design/Graphics** (creates content for advertising and web, does layout, etc.)
  - **Social Media/PR** (schedules posts/posters, creates content, manages advertising, manages social media sites, etc. Could be two people.)
  - **Web Editor** (manages actual websites, maintains and posts content, works with others on design, updating, etc.)
  - **Faculty Advisor** (institutional support, attends meetings, manages oversight, supports editors, community outreach, etc.)
  - **Graduate Assistant/Advisor** (trouble-shooting, event management support, community outreach, etc.)

Communication

- **Email Accounts** (spell them out but keep ID&PW elsewhere; how to use)
- **Meetings** (process, agenda, follow up, minutes)
- **Submission Manager** (how it's used, who has access)
- **Grievance Procedures** (staff can hit bumps with each other …)
- **Office Policies** (access, maintenance, uses and limits, etc.)
- **Updating the Manual** (who does it and when and how)

- **Forms, Contacts, and Contracts** (what they are, when they are needed—your handbook appendices can include the blank forms)
- **Staff Interviews and Transitions** (how are they conducted?)

Production Process

- **Submissions** (what you are publishing—perhaps a statement of aesthetics)
- **Guidelines for Submissions** (general policy for handling submitted work: each of the following described in terms of length, type, format)

  Fiction

  Poetry

  NonFiction

  Reviews

  Interviews

  Art

  Music

  Audio and video files

- **Solicited Submissions** (exactly what, exactly how—perhaps a policy on Contributing Editors)
- **Selection Process** (quick outline of policies on the selection process)
- **Distribution of Submissions** (who does it, when, and how)
- **Slush Meetings** (who must attend, and what happens at them)
- **Final Decisions** (who decides, and what happens with first edits)
- **Notifying Submitters** (decline and accept)
- **Policies on Revisions and Editing** (how much, when, what circumstances)
- **Collection and Processing of Accepted Work** (who does the final edits, what is needed—reference to "style sheet" rules in Appendix)
- **Layout/Design Parameters** (guidelines for the layout person)
- **Proofreading** (the process, what's needed)
- **Printing** (who you deal with, the timeline, the contact info)
- **Working with Bids and Printers** (general guidelines for new editors)
- **Printer's Proof** (what is necessary for a final approval)
- **Budget** (where financial records are kept, who has access, what's included)
- **Events** (basic outline of each type of event required annually)

- **Launch** (venue list, contacts, typical schedule, staffing needs, data collection)
- **Readings** (venue list, contacts, format, staffing needs, open mic sign up sheet, etc.)
- **Tabling** (equipment list, managing sales, record-keeping, staffing)
- **Contests, Prizes, and Awards** (schedule and parameters)
  Etc.

Office

- **Journal Inventory** (done how often, by whom, recorded where)
- **Email Manager** (who answers email, processing, updating info, etc.)
- **Contact Info for Contributors and Orders** (mailing and list maintenance)
- **Subscriptions and Distribution** (spreadsheet maintenance, subscriber lists, mailing process)
- **End of Year Report** (written by whom, submitted where, containing what)
- **Logo** (digital files with the logo and the journal typeface, images, and requirements)
- **Letterhead** (digital letterhead that can be printed as well as used digitally)

Appendixes

A. Staff Application

B. Email templates

C. Submission response templates

D. Financial Documents and Forms

E. Logos, fonts, etc.

F. Proofreading Guidelines/Style Sheet

Handbooks can also get easily out of date—if your publication grows, for instance—and they should be regularly updated by people who actually do the work. Consider it a wrap-up activity. With platforms like Google Drive you can easily file documents as PDFs and even as draft documents so everyone can edit at once. (With rules on edits, of course.) Always keep a copy of your old handbook in your archives, recorded by active dates—you might be surprised how many times an editorial staff will wonder how the staff *used* to do things. Handbooks can also be written or updated by someone else (a faculty committee, perhaps) if there are questions about rules from the department or permissions needed from the university. These are all examples of a living document which helps shape the organization but also change along with it. Every year—or few years, if the handbook seems solid—changes can be made and voted on by the staff. Not everyone is going to do the voting part, perhaps, but you know you have a solid document if you get general agreement from the staff on what the handbook should say. In between, you can always maintain a document titled something like "Handbook Notes" where everyone can write down the present thinking on something that might have to change due to staffing, financial concerns, convenience, or university policy changes.

A new handbook can start with a few simple directions:

"Poetry submissions will be read by a staff of readers under direction of the Poetry Editor." What does that direction entail? The Poetry Editor will be responsible for processing submissions: finding the properly submitted works in the submission manager, distributing them to the poetry readers [or Poetry Staff or whatever name your organization uses for those who read the slush pile], running slush meetings, deciding on final acceptances with the staff, doing first edits with the Editor-in-Chief, and contacting all the writers. Will follow the appropriate production procedures step-by-step and submit final copy to the designer.

Editorial Practices—A Quick Primer

A lot can be said about how work is chosen from a slush pile for publication—or whether you want to solicit work from writers whose work you enjoy. Below are a few quick guidelines that might be helpful at the outset:

- **Don't publish staff.** When you do this, it looks like the worst sort of nepotism, like you are taking university funds/time/attention in order to publish yourselves or your friends. Make it a policy that if an editor's friend submits a piece, the editor must reveal the connection and perhaps recuse themselves from the decision process.

- **Have a talk with the staff about what kind of work you are looking for and perhaps even use examples from previous issues of your magazine (for or against).** Talk about writers you admire and what they do that you admire (when you interview potential staff ask them about writers they enjoy and why). Keep this in mind always: "quality" is easy to claim, but it's best when you can say as clearly as possible what you are looking for in every category (fiction, poetry, nonfiction, experimental, art, etc.) Realism? Minimalism? Flash? Speculative fiction or even sci-fi and fantasy that is free of clichés, stereotypes, and common tropes. Documentary poetry or perhaps a

wide range of styles? Narrative? Experimental? Perhaps you want
surprise? Or somewhere on the highway between understatement
and pabulum?

- **Consider having your staff write reviews** (of books, movies, TV
  shows, other journals) and do interviews with writers who are not
  students—maybe try former students, visiting writers, or community
  writers who might have something to say to your readership. (Plan
  these invitations to others to write reviews or interviews, and don't
  promise publication until you see the product.)

- **Keep the readership in mind, always.** Best to know who they
  are. Yes, they are your teachers and professors and administrators,
  but mostly they are other writers like the ones you are publishing.
  Don't overcompensate on your choices by assuming you will
  encounter censorship at your institution. It is likely that you will not.
  Remember to address readers you aspire to attracting.

- **Be careful of soliciting work from known writers or artists.** What
  if they send something crappy? (It happens!) Then what are you
  going to say? (Consider asking for an interview, perhaps, rather
  than their unknown, unpublished work.) If you are attending a
  reading and hear someone read a great piece (poetry or prose) or
  happen to come across a specific unpublished work you would like
  to publish, perhaps ask the writer (check with your staff; again,
  don't promise anything) if they would be interested in submitting the
  work for consideration and be sure to give them easy, clear info for
  submitting. ("Here is a bookmark with our web address." "Send it to
  me; here is my email.")

- **Consider having Contributing Editors.** What writers would
  look good on your masthead? Contributing editors bring you the
  excellent work they find—maybe sending on their students' work
  or the writing of someone they've read with somewhere or know.
  You can ask for diverse subjects from writers typically marginalized.
  Have clearly stated rules for these "editors." Perhaps a well-known
  writer that is one of your contributing editors will agree to submit
  a piece of their own work to you once every two years and will
  submit to you the work of others twice every year. What they send
  can go directly to the Editor-in-Chief who then engages the section
  editors to decide: "Should we take this?" If you have contributing
  editors, be very on top of your communication and be sure to follow
  through on your side of "contract." When you don't take the work
  they submit, be effusive in your thanks for their effort.

- **Be very clear that you only publish work that has not yet been
  published.** Some new writers don't really understand this yet
  and may think "Oh, sure, I can publish it with you and that other
  place too …." Typically serial rights are what you are looking

for: unpublished work, where you are the first to publish, and the rights revert back to the writer after you publish. They get to do as they like after that—it's basically an honor system and it is up to them to tell the next periodical or anthology that the piece was first (already) published in your magazine. If they don't inform the next publisher? They look bad but it's on them. If they do direct a future publisher to your magazine as the original venue for their excellent work, you look really great because you found them first. If you want to publish ONLY reprints, that's another issue entirely. https://www.legalzoom.com/articles/reprinted-with-permission-getting-consent-to-republish-someone-elses-work

- **Have a clear accept/decline process.** Advertise your deadlines and keep them (or extend them, but do that widely, posting the update everywhere you posted the announcement in the first place). Make sure that all correspondence is kept for a reasonable amount of time. (Archive the organization's email but don't throw it out for a year at least.) Be VERY direct in your correspondence and make sure you clear the submissions before you go on to the next issue. Your rejections (such a harsh word!) can be phrased nicely. Don't be afraid to say no and don't invite someone to submit again later if you don't really mean it.

- **Do not accept work conditionally**—especially based on future edits. Let's say a poem or story is quite good but has one very major flaw. Maybe two or three flaws. The story needs a new ending? The poem has a weird line in the middle? What makes you think the writer will see what you see, understand it the way you do, and actually make it better? (Believe me, you will often get something worse—being under a watchful eye and having fast deadlines can cause such pressure that writers simply blank out or do their level best and toss it back your way.) You can always give a writer feedback (but you can't do this in every case—you will wear yourselves out doing this) and suggest they resubmit next year (if they are eligible) or simply wish them luck in their writing endeavors. If you clearly want to cut only a short bit, you certainly can ask the writer, but know what your answer is, ahead of time, if they say no. Always give the writer a deadline for responding to your edits or ideas, and when that deadline has just passed, write a very polite note that you are (a) moving on or (b) giving them one more day (or the weekend).

- **Honor the process, don't undermine it.** One of the best things about being an editor (well, one of the two best things) is seeing how manuscripts get processed. You get to see what happens to YOUR creative work when it arrives at a publication for review. The other best thing is reading enough of other people's work that you get an idea of what is out there, what other people are doing with their writing. You will find out that a grandparent poem is a real thing (it should not stop you from writing one, but it is a thing). It might be finally, totally clear to you that a cliché is a dangerous thing to waste.

- **Check your edits and be consistent.** When working with writers on final edits, you are mostly making sure all the punctuation is correct or that the capital letters on certain words are consistent. So many little things need an eagle eye. One could make a very long list of very simple things like "Is that supposed to be Ernie talking in the middle of page 5, or Grace?" But let's stop here: the section editors, while choosing their favorite pieces in a slush meeting with their reading staff, can easily mark up a primary manuscript with editing questions or suggestions. They can collect and collate potential changes, perhaps checking with a comanaging or other editor on what they think needs to be done before they send the list of corrections/questions/changes to the writer for final edits. Remember: you should always check with the writer on edits. And save that correspondence—it is proof, later, if there are questions about what was agreed upon. Do not ever make assumptions or changes without asking. DO read carefully and ask questions. Organize the comments you send to the writer so they can be dealt with directly. Often the turnaround time has to be quick.

- **Keep records safely, save account info.** You are likely to have a plethora of online accounts—email, submission managers, bank accounts, etc. Keep your records—emails, IDs and passwords, marked manuscripts, always updated and available *to the people who need to have access.* That means keeping them in more than one place, probably, with extra caution for the more sensitive information (things like bank accounts and your websites—too many cooks on the website can cause problems).

Your journal will have to decide on how egalitarian or democratic it is going to be. There are advantages and disadvantages to each structure. (Most student organizations are a mix of both.) Either way, when final decisions are made, when feedback is put to action, when problems have to be addressed, the Editor-in-Chief is frequently the voice that speaks a final decision and has to check up to see that others follow through. This does not make everyone happy. (Some decisions make no one happy.) Leadership can be hard. A good faculty advisor or graduate advisor can help support any student editor when that student is doing their best to turn a fragile situation into something (hopefully) less bad. Be available. Listen. Step in only when the students can't solve the matter themselves.

Diversity

A truly diverse organization should at the very least reflect the diversity of the college's or university's student body. That's the bare minimum. Better to go wider, perhaps. We often think of diversity as the usual: race, ethnicity, gender, sexual orientation, socioeconomic status, age, physical (dis)abilities, religious beliefs, and perhaps political beliefs. But there are other matters of identity as well, and it can be an enlightening experience to listen to students, staff, and faculty to find out how they would define diversity. Each of those diversities mentioned above is also not one thing, nor do they represent one viewpoint. In other words, be curious and get to know each other. Invite people in and you will have the advantage of their skills or ideas. Perhaps there are students who don't have their own computer equipment or internet access (perhaps they will have ideas of how to connect with others in this situation) and some students who own their own companies (they might have great office organization ideas). Some may not have access to transportation while others have two jobs and children to raise. Others are in their thirties and never held a job. You may have a wealthy student with particular views on how money works who agrees completely with a student on scholarship about organizing the budget. All of these different lenses brought to the literary magazine will help you produce a better result—if you can figure out how to run an organization that honors the voices of many. This means that not everyone is always running everything—there is simply no way to include every view in every decision. It does mean figuring out where the skills and willingness are located. Remember, decisions constantly made by a system that favors lowest common denominator (everyone must agree), or decisions that constantly fall to the same small group of people, can get quite dull.

The tech industry sometimes uses the acronym "EDI" for equity, diversity, and inclusion. While you can make your own definitions for each of those terms (it's a good exercise), you might start with equity as a plan, diversity as an outcome, and inclusion as action. You might plan to give everyone equal access to opportunities at every level, you actively include a variety of people to contribute as you work, and you look at what you've done and measure how diverse the result is. The acronym basically reminds you to be aware, all the time.

Listening to and instituting good ideas from the margins can really help an organization shine. *Because there is wealth all around you.* Try actually following the lead of those who rarely speak—not just giving someone airtime but figuring out how to include their input by moving several steps in that direction. Consider everyone's initial input valuable because it is—everyone's voice is the voice of the group as it forms. Listen, and give everyone a chance to work their personal magic somewhere.

Diversity of the organization's staff requires a workplace vibe of humble interest in the creative process via various paths. Different voices should

One fall semester—new staff, new academic year—I watched an editing staff determine that they could work together even though the group members' political viewpoints were widely different. They went forward with good intent. As the year wore on and questions about comments and editing choices were processed and noted again and again, it became…less easy. Micro aggressions were frequently mentioned in communications and meetings. The different parties wanted a reckoning, seeing their own complaints as the most valid. The discussions did not go well and the students no longer trusted each other. I suggested they all recommit to the work at hand: focus on the journal and events. The graduate student advisor listened, too, and steered the students to their best practices—as well as the disagreeing parties could implement them. We both pointed out that taking offense could be as easy as being offensive—hoping everyone could learn something here, including us. By the end of the academic year, despite attempts to change course, the two camps could hardly speak to each other. When it came to choosing new staff for the coming year, we chose to not offer positions to any applicants who flatly refused to work with others.

allow any single person to see beyond their own limits, which everyone has. An ability to consider (and honor) the contributions of those differently abled—and to know our own strengths and weaknesses—this creates progress. In other words, it might seem dangerous to say something new, or ask a seemingly obvious question, but speak up! Let your working group know what's on your mind. As a member of the group, or as the leader, you can make the workspace a better place by encouraging conversation on just about anything. Trust each other a bit. Don't forget to take the extra time to listen. And always consider the functionality and accessibility of what you are doing—both in terms of "doing" physically and in terms of varied viewpoints.

It's true that occasionally, when people don't listen to each other, the spinning wheels of nondecision or mere stubbornness can bog down the works. Remember that it's not just listening to different ideas: the group has to *act* from the position of diversity. The leadership has to BE diverse. Everyone has to adjust sometimes and solutions might not speak to every single person in the organization, but trying something different will often provide a good lesson and sometimes a fantastic outcome. It doesn't mean that the organization will always try to do everything that everyone suggests (and if you can't let go of the fear of failing, you probably shouldn't be doing this work anyway), but it does mean that you have to change up the way you see things, as individuals, so that more opinions are heard and acted upon. It doesn't mean that you constantly second guess yourselves, or ignore the obvious or dismiss truth, but it does mean you are always self-aware and try to learn from others. It doesn't mean stereotyping anyone, though it does mean taking differences into account (and valuing what those differences bring to the project, even if it's complicated). It doesn't mean thanking people constantly for simply showing up (the product is theirs too—"thank you" might imply that they are doing something for you, personally, when the outcome belongs to all), but it does mean recognizing excellent input/ work and giving credit to the people who brought the ideas forward and to the people who did the work. These are not always the same people.

Here's another, related nagging problem: undergraduate magazines are often thought of as a clique-ish kind of club house. Perhaps this is because the organization is there to make value judgments on other people's creative work and that's a bit scary for the other writers around who are not on staff. In my experience, the students I've worked with have more often *not* known each other before we started, though by the end many have become friends. (Honestly, producing an art project—which a website or print magazine is, basically—with a collective purpose, brings people together in a work environment like nothing else I've ever seen.) Still, the focus on the work can be misunderstood as the dismissal of those who are standing by. Remember to look around, acknowledge the contributors and audience, and ask for feedback. Even the appearance of an "inside group" can discourage others from submitting work or being involved, so take opportunities to reach out and include others. Literally, say hello and ask for feedback. It can be particularly helpful to involve staff members—from the outset, the sooner the better—who seem different (or are from other departments like business, art, theater, technology). Bring in people you don't know, people you have to approach and ask to join. Don't be afraid. You may get to know them! (And they you.) Would they be interested in working with a mixed group, or a wall of sameness? Can the group coalesce around a guiding vision of what's ahead? If you ever hear the voice inside your head making clear distinctions between "us" and "them"—it's time to reconsider your work in terms of lack of diversity. Invite some distinction through discussion.

When it comes to the diversity of the selections your editorial groups make (the selection of written work or artwork), you have to first consider what your magazine is doing and why (see Chapter 1). Looking for the "best" work is far too easy to say. Who owns the perfect lens on what "best" is? Qualities are involved. (Note that I did not say "quality"—that's only one thing. The qualities, plural, would be determined by your clear list of desired elements in the work, the qualities you are looking for, and your aesthetic.) Your ideas, your writers' guidelines, and your editorial practices really have to work together and create a recognizable, workable process. If you want poetry that uses imagery but moves beyond the image or narrative to make meaning, spell that out. If you like experimental work, try not to use the word "original" because that is an undue burden. You may want work that favors uncommon subjects—or extremely pedestrian moments. Spend some

What kind of diversity can an editor look for in the journal's submissions? A poetry editor reads a poem that might be described as an identity poem—and the language turns angry at the end. Or at least it seems so to the poetry editor who liked the poem but thought it worked better with the last three lines removed. "I feel more comfortable with it this way." Hmm. Are poems supposed to avoid discomfort? Maybe there are not any artful missteps in the last three lines. Who is asking whom to change what? Consider. On the other hand, another editor seems to choose ONLY identity pieces and does not seem to consider work that appears to be about other topics though the writer appears to belong to an underrepresented group. This is, perhaps, a subcategory of stereotyping. Don't insist that your views of difference be the only ones represented. If you don't understand a piece, ask yourself why and see if you might learn something about language or craft or about people—by sitting with the work, discussing, or researching. Always be honest with yourself about your tools (or lack thereof) as an arbiter.

time with the group (or subsection of readers on staff) discussing the kinds of creative work that you admire. Avoid appropriation in your selections for publication—discuss what that means and get your slush pile readers oriented to questioning texts that seem to lean on tropes and stereotypes or that are doing a lot of questionable cultural "borrowing." Be careful of making assumptions about writers based on their names or other limited info.

Establishing an Annual Schedule

Production deadlines are necessary—the work has to get done in reasonable fashion. The staff might want to weigh in on what "reasonable" means by looking broadly at the work/exam/course schedule for the coming year. Include the section editors, those involved in various aspects of the organization, when putting together the annual schedule. More eyes make for a more complete, successful workflow. Call a meeting, keep focused. At the very beginning of the academic year—or the end of the academic year that results in the new staff and Editor-in-Chief being chosen—put together the relevant people (and be generous here—include the faculty advisor who knows a little more about how the university works, and/or the graduate advisor who might be on the hook to help out) and open up both last year's calendar along with a blank calendar for the year ahead. Take a deep breath. Look at everything.

I suggest using Google Calendars so that the information can be accessed anytime by anyone on staff. While you are putting together the calendar, everyone at the meeting can see and edit a Google calendar as you go; all of

Time management was a crucial skill for us to have—both as managing editors and also for the journal at large. There are lots of moving parts—deadlines to be met, people to coordinate with, teams to supervise in editing and layout—and one piece falling behind schedule could throw the whole process out of whack. So understanding how to make a schedule and stick to it on both an individual and group scale was important.

— Amy Elizabeth Bishop, Co-Managing
Editor *Gandy Dancer* Spring 2015

you can access it later to check in or make updates; whatever you do at an annual scheduling meeting, do not delete the previous year's calendar as that may be the reference point you will need later. (Archive previous calendars for a few years—you might be surprised how often you have to reach back more than a year to figure out what exact event, when, who, etc.)

Make a list of all the things that need to be done in the coming year (again, using last year's calendar and pondering for a moment on how well that worked) and begin by scheduling your biggest and toughest events: the date the magazine has to go to the printer or be posted online (in order to be ready for a launch party before the end of the semester); the last possible award announcement date, the reading that has to take place before spring break (or after), etc. Then work back from there. What's the last possible date to have readers lined up for that first reading of the semester? How much time do the sections need to get through the slush pile? Back up from there: when should the advertising for submissions start? How long does it take to proofread the next issue and how long does your designer need to input all the corrections after the proofreading is done? If you are using judges for your contest, how much time do you give the final judges to make a decision? (Based, no doubt, on the number of entries you are giving them.) As you work backward (and forward), take notes. Remember to check the university's or college's calendar and be mindful of national holidays. Have many eyes on this calendar process because more eyes means it's less likely that something has been skipped or entered twice or that a conflict (exams!) has arisen.

On the subject of conflicts, the greatest challenge you will face is staffing and time limits. Many people are donating their time, and, in a pinch, they may have to skip an event or a task. Sometimes at the last moment. The conflicts can be wide-ranging (some are not avoidable—people fall ill, earthquakes and floods happen). If an editor has to work for a living, that might have to be taken into account on scheduling regular staff meetings. When are midterms, finals? Spring Break? If many people are involved in the schedule-building process, they become invested and might be more likely to inform the group when something changes in their lives. Again, including a multitude can seem cumbersome when first establishing a schedule of activities and deadlines, but might mean much smoother running as time goes by. Everyone feels included. Everyone makes adjustments and pitches in when they feel their investment in the organization matters. When staff knows what goes into scheduling, they may be able to see the road ahead more clearly. Communication is, again, essential.

Consider also the potential conflicts with related partners at the university. There might be schedule conflicts with other department events—be sure to get someone in the department's front office (or the chair—they may have the most complete calendar for department events) to give you a list of dates for other events being planned or already confirmed. You might send an email request for a preliminary list of potential dates—well before you meet to create a schedule. Certainly keep the university's or college's academic calendar nearby while scheduling.

Inevitably things will change and adjustments will have to be made. Be generous (or put your foot down) when it's appropriate. In most cases it's no one's fault. And when there is an error, a very thorough calendar can help the staff adjust themselves or even adjust a few dates affected by a change. A good calendar up front—one that also includes dates for social media posts and emails, email contact reminders, etc.—can help everyone move the organization forward.

Communication

Spend some time thinking about the flow of communication within your organization and outside the editorial space. How do you want to come across? Writers are language oriented—how obvious is that?—so you might expect to find this communication part easy, right? Rarely does communication happen seamlessly. Gaps happen, misunderstanding occurs. It takes quite a bit of intention and practice to move around gracefully. This is another reason why your archives will be useful, as patterns of what to do or not do. I will also mention—or should I say repeat?—the part about having a few people look at any text/ad copy the organization disseminates in order to check for accuracy and errors. And tone.

Some say that what you don't know won't kill you—unless you are trying to run an arts organization. Whether it's within the organization or reaching toward the larger writing/arts community, too many gaps in the flow of information, too many missed opportunities, and things fall apart. You don't respond? People won't include you. An advisor I know had a situation in which the journal editor knew a literary festival had been cancelled (she'd received an email) but she neglected to tell anyone else. The students went ahead, got organized, and drove an hour through a snow storm.

You can't let the staff feel left out, disregarded, and disrespected—all because the flow of information is uncertain or spotty. Not because anyone did anything intentionally mean, of course not. There has to be a basic and consistent flow of information—a weekly meeting (with an agenda sent ahead) or biweekly informational email (with updates), perhaps. A regular system for reminders. A document everyone can check for status updates. You can also use Slack or Teams or similar office software. Something to focus everyone's attention and disseminate important information.

Best to create a space for staff members to make friends for life. Between the highs and lows is where most literary organizations survive, functioning well enough and catching a few snags. Don't be afraid to apologize, and good things can happen when everyone is included in discussions on how to recover. Need to celebrate a big success? Do it! (Recently our graduate advisor invited the upper editors to celebrate some work well done by playing Dungeons and Dragons—I think she led them on an all-weekend binge.)

The flow of information top-down can work, at meetings, but when everyone is invited to contribute during those meetings, good decisions are strengthened. I cannot stress how pro-conning a decision or idea with the group can result in a better outcome. (Especially when things don't work out and later everyone returns to the dissenter to say "Okay! We are trying your way next time on this!") Beyond the group of upper editors, however, each section will need its own communication structure. Each section editor will probably establish their own mode of crucial communication for their subgroup, of course, but there are a few things you can start with to make things run more smoothly for everyone, regardless.

Upper editors should have a list of all upper editors' emails and phone numbers (along with the advisors). Same with section editors and their reading staff. (Make sure everyone knows that you never—never never ever—give out someone's private contact info without asking them first. Ever.) You might establish a communication blueprint by suggesting some basic rules for editors contacting each other: first contact is through a communication manager or email, then text, and only in emergencies make a call. There are those excellent communication platforms I've mentioned that help you manage everyday communication and keep your email inboxes a bit clearer. But you must check them. Your university might even have a license for an online communication platform. Teams, for instance, got a lot more popular in the recent pandemic. It is part of the Microsoft suite that many universities and colleges purchase for general use.

Communicating was probably the most important thing I asked the prose readers to do. I always started with 20 or more readers and anticipated that some would end up feeling overwhelmed with school and some would stop replying to my reminders entirely. When they told me they were unable to make it to an event or couldn't read a certain number of pieces they'd been assigned, it was never an issue as long as I wasn't told at the last minute. We always had enough people to handle the load as long as everyone was upfront with me.

–Francesca Ervin, Prose Editor *Glass Mountain* 2016–2017

The main thing about communication is that it has to be direct (you have a question, then ask it—no blah blah) and clear (be specific). No fussing around, polite language only, and keep in mind that simple sentences (emails and texts) can seem a bit sharp. When something seems a little cutting or abrupt it probably has nothing to do with you. Everyone has a life. Give everyone a little space. Assume the best. Focus on the work. Be gentle, even if others aren't. And keep an eye on the calendar—let someone know about a response timeline. In your messaging, include everyone who needs to know.

That last part can be a little tricky. Some people are very sensitive about being too, uhm, well informed. (This is where Teams or Slack can come in useful—the info is there for everyone to see and no one has to feel bothered, though everyone must check in regularly for these sites to work effectively. Download the app on your phone. Turn on/off notifications as appropriate.) If someone is bothered by another staff member's communication (or lack thereof) you might also have a handbook policy about consistent problems: do you go to the managing editor if there's a complaint? The Editor-in-Chief? As a faculty advisor I am often the last to know, but once the students come to me the exact nature of the problem is usually pretty clear. Sometimes the Title IX office gets involved. Mostly a quick conversation (and some agreement between the persons involved) clears things up. And I always check back to see how things are going. In other words, create the expectation that people should try to work out solutions amongst themselves. And don't be afraid to bring things up with the intent of helping them figure it out. People often don't mean to come across as short or stupid or mean or daft. If you speak up and remain respectful, you can probably help everyone be more effective. Once everyone understands where people are coming from, things get a lot easier.

So speak up. Believe me, the best work is done when everyone can count on open communication that is respectful and addresses a common goal.

The communicating the organization does with writers and readers, your department or college, the student activities office, Development or Admissions, and literary organizations outside of the literary magazine is usually much easier because there are professional standards concerning polite discourse. Most communications are rather formal—direct, courteous, and efficient. General rules about style and form apply: plain sentences with clear information, quick opening and closing (usually with contact info). The tone and style of an award announcement is perhaps more dry and somewhat formal while a Call for Submissions can use snappier language, some humor, maybe less formal verbiage. In the latter case you are composing a fun invitation. In the former, you are officially honoring work well done. Whatever the purpose, you have to gauge the intent of your message, take into account your audience, and match the language with the outcome you want. Know your audience, of course, but also consider how you want to come across. Your language represents you, right? Of course your communication style is also another way to use your skills as a writer: be creative and provide your target audience with a good reason to engage.

Micro aggressions. Our speech belies our viewpoints, whether we like it or not. Habits can be changed, awareness can help. When staff members can't get along, however, everything begins to sound like a criticism. Defensiveness can sound like criticism. You might have to have an open dialogue on the problem in order to hit the reset button. In other cases (and please look carefully at the difference), a staff member might be taking their social privilege—whatever that consists of in that context—for granted. They don't seem to listen, don't seem to understand that their language is insensitive, or can't seem to imagine that there is another way to experience the world and to process the messaging. Taking a sensitive approach to insensitivity can seem...counterintuitive? But it's a place to start. If a couple of friendly souls can quietly speak with the Clueless One and guide them into a new land of social skills via gentle and direct dialogue, that's great. Everyone has to learn and relearn social skills. After all, social skills are received—made by example. If that doesn't work, try the direct approach: stop them in their tracks and ask them to explain what they mean. Try to do this in a safe place and/or with another person present. Simply tell them what you hear them saying. Take a deep breath. Stay calm. Listen and speak with compassion. If you need to remove yourself from the situation, excuse yourself and do so. Maybe try calling in before you try calling out.

You also have to answer your email. Have a set of policies for dealing with what appears in the organization's inbox. If there is one email address for the organization, consider having the managing editor be the one person who opens the messages and then puts them in the relevant mailbox (set up according to editing sections or peoples' names) for further actions. Have some guidelines for flagging an email needing immediate response versus what constitutes an email that's in a holding pattern (waiting for further info perhaps). Everyone has to do their part to keep the email account operating smoothly, so establish some ground rules on response times for general inquiries or orders for merchandise. Don't leave anything too long—if there is going to be a lag time on the reply (you might have to figure out who mailed that order, and when), you can send a quick message that you are looking into the issue and will be responding in detail soon. Then do that. (See below on email exchanges with writers during production.) Put together a general policy on saving, deleting, and especially archiving email. Write down your email processing policy—put it in the handbook. Make sure everyone sticks to the policy with regular reminders.

It's also a good idea to have one person respond to all outside inquiries—as a representative of the organization (usually a managing editor). This gives a regular and competent voice to the organization. This person would, for instance, have the schedule at hand for reference ("Thank you for the invitation but we have another event that day") as well as the Editor-in-Chief's ear in case there is a larger issue. ("We would rather attend that event but we already said yes to this event, so now what do we do? Maybe we can send a smaller contingent to both events. Let's ask the staff.") There should always be a ready way to contact outside organizations (and the staff) as well as a designated person to reach out so things aren't done twice or not at all. Your organization can always keep a spreadsheet (an internal communication tracker) for everyone's use. That way you can all keep track of what has gone out and when.

Keeping a file of email/posting templates in your archive or Google Drive folder can help too—as mentioned elsewhere here, there is no need for each person to reinvent the entire wheel on a semiannual submission announcement, for instance. If you plan on doing a contest every year, by all means keep those announcement/poster/email files in a place that's easy to find next year.

What about communication software like Mailchimp? Excellent question! Marketing platforms like Mailchimp are wonderful tools, but also take time to maintain and can cost some money. As I have pointed out, there is a free version that offers fewer services but those can be helpful enough to small magazines—check it out. You can use Mailchimp to make fantastic-looking emails. Of course you must maintain a platform like Mailchimp, or your account hangs there as something you sort of own but can't effectively use and that is a drag on the organization. ("Oh, right—did anyone update the email lists last semester …?") Maintenance can mean simple, regular updating or a more comprehensive reconfiguring (if you find that some contact info is out of date or not appropriate for that list anymore, etc.)—or anything in between. The communication software programs that are free for certain limited uses have distinct rules. MailChimp, for instance, can only be used with the permission of the recipient. You can't just input email addresses you've scrubbed from the nearby university's website, for instance. (You can, however, make your own spreadsheet of emails you've found, people whom you would like to reach out to for specific purposes—you can email them directly, just not through MailChimp.) While a service like MailChimp can make your email messages more professional and readable, you do have to work at it a bit. There are design choices they provide, though having recent cover art ready for uploading will make the emails more attractive and present tense. For announcements it's rather easy to include your logo, your journal's name and typeface, a banner, or a photo.

And how about multiple email addresses? Does your university or college provide your literary magazine with email accounts?—and maybe a software program to manage that email? (As mentioned, you can always use Gmail, for free—for the moment, at least.) Careful of too many email accounts floating around out there—your organization may have used an old email to buy a domain name, open a bank account, who knows! Thinking forward, make sure that any accounts you open that

An upper editing team is just that—a team. No team can be its most effective if it's made up of a group of loosely-linked strangers, so my advice as a former editor-in-chief is to make time for team bonding! Making time to do things unrelated to the task at hand may seem silly when there are approximately one million other things that need to be done for production, but the better a team knows how each other operates (works, has fun, laughs, cries, even), the smoother the rest will go.

–Melinda Mayden, Editor-in-Chief, *Glass Mountain Magazine*, 2019–2020

have email addresses attached are recorded somewhere safe so future editors can find what they need. Your university may have a policy about using outside email addresses for university functions. (Again, this is where the student activities office can probably help you, for information on the legal and or "customary" practices of student groups who are a part of the institution but operate separately in particular ways—like reaching out to other nonprofits in your area.) Whatever you do, don't open email accounts all over the place or use the private email of an editor for the business of the group. Gmail is ubiquitous at the moment, but a university email address will have the support of IT services and that can be very helpful, too.

Be sure to have different sizes and resolutions for your logo, your logo and journal name, and just your journal name—there should be a signature typeface for the name. Make sure the logo and name can work in black and white—it will make your life easier. The different resolutions and sizes will work in different applications—an email, a poster design, the web, the layout. Need a logo? Find the art department, the graphics team, and collect several possibilities before you choose. Same thing with letterhead—have a variety of designs for specific uses. But once you choose the logo and the name of the journal with signature typeface, don't change it up. Be consistent. Be recognizable.

Production and Design

Putting a new issue together is pretty intense. The fiction section groans under the weight of so many short stories and so many opinions on which are best. The poetry section is looking for ... how many poems for the next issue? Or is it how many *pages* of poetry? (There's a real difference between those two.) Perhaps questions arise on how the art was chosen. Are selections beginning to all sound/look similar? That music file you wanted to add is actually a "performance piece" that doesn't work as audio only. As explained in other places in this book, good communication, a schedule, and a clear purpose will help keep processes on track and make an easier path for everyone through production.

Before you even consider the production schedule, the entire group should be clear on the intent and purpose for the coming issue. Checking in with each other part way through the reading process might help you find a continuous thread in the selections. You could plan ahead for a themed issue. Perhaps there is a design or style choice (there may be a space limitation or an online design consideration) that will affect what each section chooses to include in the publication. Writing down your objectives for the coming issue—or keeping a file where the final selections go so others can read them—will help keep everyone focused on the material they are bringing into production.

Here is a quick general chronology of what happens during production:

- **Open your submission period** (with clear guidelines and a specific deadline)
- **Advertise** for submissions
- Section editors **check the submission manager** and **distribute submissions** to slush-pile readers regularly
- **Keep advertising** for submissions
- **Check in with each section** (are submissions being processed?) and send out deadline reminders—post notices and changes on your website, send emails to each other to update on progress
- (Do you want to extend the deadline? Advertise the extension!)
- Close to deadline, **check with staff on how well the reading process is going**: are they finding the material they want? Are submissions being processed as planned? Are there any problems?
- **Have a slush meeting not too long after the deadline**—distribute all the submissions before that meeting. (You can send rejections as you go or send them all at once when you finalize a roster of submissions that will work for your next issue. Careful of rejecting too much too fast.)
- **Start advertising for the launch event** (as you continue advertising, you may list some of the writers selected for this issue as readers at your launch)
- **Make decisions on final choices** (perhaps ranked, in case there are pieces that turn out to be unavailable) after you check with the Editor-in-Chief and managing editor on available space for each section; deal with any other questions about submissions (too long, too short, too similar, too dark/funny/experimental/sentimental/standard etc.) with the editors together

- **Contact the writers/artists and work on final edits** once there is a green light on the selected pieces from the Editor-in-Chief (or the group has decided to proceed with the choices)—there is a sample Acceptance Letter in Appendix B
- **Choose cover art or web page design art** (or any art submissions)
- **Sequencing:** once all fully edited material is collected and ready, have the upper editors meet for sequencing (the order in which pieces appear in a physical book or on a website's architecture/ design map—discussed later)
- **Send the plan/map/directives, along with the fully edited text/ art/sound/video files, to your layout person**
- **Proofreading—section readers go over materials in layout files/ pages**—checking every word, margin, line, color, bio, table of contents, etc. for correctness
- **Send your layout files to the printer or have your web designer show staff the layout of the web pages with a URL that isn't live**
- **For printing, get the printer's proof and check one last time for any errors** they may have made or corrections you might want to make (it might cost a little money if you made the errors—but this is your chance to fix them; for websites, **get your proofreaders combing the pages one last time for any necessary adjustments/ corrections/redesign**
- **Send out reminders for the launch**: amplify those writers/artists!
- **Let the writers/artists know their pieces are posted online or send complimentary copies of the printed volume**
- **Celebrate!** and repeat.

Let's get more specific on each step—keeping in mind that this is still a very general way of describing production. Your process, your situation, will no doubt be different as you work with what you have and what it is you want to ultimately do. Borrow what you need from this list and create the rest. No doubt, however, on this one thing: you should have a clear plan and clear dates before you start. Draw up a production schedule well before the start of the semester. Don't even consider starting production without everyone involved having access to deadlines and dates. Have an agreed-upon scheduled meeting for final selections, for layout, for proofreading … for everything! (If production is part of a class, this is probably all on the syllabus.) Dates that you've set ahead of time can probably be moved around a little (you can never tell—weather and humans being themselves), but do not start without an absolutely clear map of the road ahead and make sure the whole staff has access to those dates/deadlines/calendars. Be prepared to make accommodations. You will quickly find out who is willing to step up and fill a gap.

Philip Levine talks about "poetry eternal" and "poetry temporal." "Poetry eternal" is how your work is in conversation with Emily Dickinson; "poetry temporal" is how a poet manages to eat. Undergraduates who are reading the slush pile with us get to see what people are writing right now. Very quickly they see that writers make the same mistakes again and again—so they learn about a terrible cliché or about some other mistake they just made when they thought they were being clever in their creative writing class. That's language—the "eternal." But they also learn how decisions are made at lit journals, and they learn about other lit mags, aesthetics, cover letters, prizes—a lot of the "temporal" stuff. All of this knowledge is incredibly valuable to each young editor, as a writer.

—Wayne Miller, Professor and Editor, *Copper Nickel*,
University of Colorado, Denver

Gathering Submissions

After you have decided what you want to publish, write up the magazine's submission guidelines. You can find these on any literary magazine's website or submission page. Make your directions as clear and simple as possible: manuscript/file format, length, style (as we've discussed, be as clear as you can about your aesthetics), resolution (for art) or file size (sound), etc. Have a submission manager ready. Submittable is commonly used for literary magazines but there are other submission managers you can purchase—your university might even have a place where students can upload their work. You can design a submission manager yourself (people have), but that is a lot of work and not suggested. Are you asking for a short bio up front, a cover letter, a fee? Perhaps you will take simultaneous submissions (where a writer sends one piece to several magazines at one time—which is quite common), but you may also ask for "notification if the piece becomes unavailable." (It is also common for new writers to neglect this step; you will likely discover that a writer has not informed you that the piece was accepted elsewhere, two months ago, and then you have to figure out how to politely say "Well, we are sorry to hear that" and not post their name on a wall in the office with a sharp tack.) Post your guidelines on your website at least, and on your Submittable pages if you can afford Submittable—or keep them just on Submittable. Your submission guidelines must be correct and updated. Provide the link in your emails and postings, and be very clear about the deadline on your website—especially when it is coming close or been extended.

A note about student literary magazines and deadlines: While setting the deadline for a specific issue (Issue #12) on a specific day (March 3rd at midnight) you can also take submissions all year. That way you can

Students learn how to write submission letters when they work on a journal. When they read submissions they'll find that they're not interested in the writer's cat or dog or even where the writer went to school. Some of the best submission letters are very short: "Here are five poems and if you publish one of them it will be my first publication." That's a perfectly good submission letter from an unpublished writer.
—Wayne Miller, Professor and Editor, *Copper Nickel*, University of Colorado, Denver

capture more submissions, remind people about that fact in any email or announcement, and generally be available to writers. This can all be spelled out on the website's submission page. You will not want to do this, obviously, if you are getting too many submissions. If you are getting too many submissions that are not appropriate (meaning submissions that you clearly will not print, that are far from the mark of what you are looking for) then you might have to revise your submission guidelines and be a little clearer about what it is you want.

Now, where are you going to advertise for submissions once you have set a deadline? Social Media is obvious (your Social Media or PR person will have their own calendar of due dates for advertising), and there are websites that list literary magazines—like NewPages, which even has a section listing undergraduate magazines (https://www.newpages.com/magazines/undergrad-lit-mags) where you can also buy advertising. You can buy ads on any number of literary-oriented websites (Duotrope is another, *Poets and Writers*, too) but be cautious about the cost and the dates. (When is your ad posted and do the dates meet reasonably with your deadline?) You might get a deal on advertising since you are a student journal. Be sure to ask. Get your email lists fired up and make sure you use the free avenues of announcement too—send emails or postings through your department or college offices. Get a poster printed up and hang them all over campus (and other community posting boards if you are looking for local writers; coffee places are a good start; community literary partners can be notified via email, of course). You might have to get permission for hanging posters, by the way. All of this advertising activity means having several reach-outs for each issue. Perhaps there's an initial call, a half-way-point reminder, a week-before reminder, and a day-before reminder. Most of your submissions will probably arrive within forty-eight hours of the deadline. If you see that you really haven't gotten the submissions you'd hoped for, you might have to extend the deadline: go back and update with anyone you've advertised with already, if possible, and then reach farther into your bag of tricks: a Facebook campaign, perhaps, if you want more community submissions. If you are an in-house publication, perhaps offer a prize (a book?) to the

When you are processing submissions, reading and deciding what pieces you would like to publish, keep in mind that the work you like best has a slate of key qualities. Be honest about that. Try to describe those qualities in your own words, keeping in mind the facts about subject, format, and style—this is your aesthetic. If you think your aesthetic is actually wider and more inclusive than your selections honestly are, you might have to do some work on your selection process—and your aesthetic.

100th person who submits before the deadline. Imagine what will work for the people you are interested in hearing from and the situation you have to work with.

If you can be very direct with your guidelines in the first place, that's best: "We are looking for speculative fiction, experimental poetry, and experience-based nonfiction." See Chapter 1 on creating your aesthetic.

If you have a design editor, you can also create messages and postings that really grab attention. Use your logo, your colors—at *Glass Mountain* we had an annual color for our Boldface Conference logo (a typewriter) which actually helped us keep track of year-to-year activities: "That's turquoise, so it must be from 2015." Whatever you have that points to your activities. You are not just advertising to get writers to submit, but to get readers in the future and new writers, eventually, too. Include links in your ads (and emails) to the guidelines or submission page or home page. Your notifications should make it very easy, even exciting, for writers to make a connection with your magazine.

Processing Submissions

Once the submissions start showing up in your submission manager, your section editors and readers must get to work pretty fast. More is coming, right up to the last minutes of the deadline. Distributing submissions to your slush pile reading staff should not be difficult—it's only the first step, so start early. Check in with your section before you start. "Ready?" How many pieces can your readers handle in a week? Ask them. (Make sure they clear their calendars for the couple of weeks *after* the deadline—everything must be read in a reasonably short period of time for most student journals.) What about your criteria for reviewing the slush pile? Are you asking that the staff read the whole submission before scoring, or only a few lines or paragraphs? (Submittable has a built-in scoring system that can help with gauging initial interest—a section editor can see if the section readers are generally or overwhelmingly interested in a piece.) How many readers per piece? (Two or three high scores will get everyone's

If a story or poem is "almost there," you can always let the writer know, right away and very politely, why the piece got rejected. Not a lot of magazines give feedback, but if the problem is obvious and can be pointed out quickly and easily—and someone on staff wants to do it—why not? (You might run the message by the Editor-in-Chief before you send any comments.) I once received an effusive thank you note from a writer when I sent a rejection with a response re: the title of her piece (I think it had "tits" in the title, and there was nothing in the piece that had anything to do with tits) needed to more accurately reflect the tone and subject of her piece. While we didn't publish it, she reported that she received a good placement for the story after she changed the title.

attention. Consistent low scores are easy to deal with too.) Section editors have to check in daily, after the deadline, to see how things are moving along. But you never actually know for certain, until you start reading, if you are getting what you had hoped to find. The section editor and readers should start reading well before the deadline, really as soon as submissions start showing up.

Avoid making final decisions too early—though you may find something that everyone agrees should be accepted, absolutely, and you might consider contacting the writer soon before the piece is taken elsewhere. Discuss with the Editor-in-Chief, faculty advisor, or other upper editors.

The final reading period (before and after deadline) can be a little stressful for the magazine, to be honest. Essentially you are trying to strike a balance between finding what you want and getting decisions made—while several other sections are doing the same thing. For instance the fiction section might get overwhelmed with good submissions while the nonfiction section doesn't have enough submissions—so do you advertise during the final week for more submissions, or perhaps only for nonfiction? The poetry section, meanwhile, didn't specify too well what they were actually looking for and the submissions are heavily weighted toward break-up poems. (Before you add "no break up poems, please" to the guidelines, is there perhaps another way you can say it? "Form is fine but no greeting-card verses, please. Heartbreak works best on park benches." Honestly, however, when you shut down subject matter, you also shut down creativity. If you can be a little humorous, the aesthetic might still be clear enough to writers.) Having your section editors checking in with the Editor-in-Chief and managing editor, regularly, can help keep things on track and provide enough time for a few quick moves before the deadline, actions that might help shape the issue in the final days of the submission period and the first days of the final reading period.

Another consideration: look over everything holistically. If you have a lot of really good artwork that's come in, perhaps you can make more room for art and cut pages for nonfiction. Work your best magic with what you have. If one section is stuck and can't make decisions, the Editor-in-Chief or managing editor can perhaps step in to keep them moving along. If there is a problem between sections, maybe with determining how much space is devoted to the genres—don't let a lot of good writing go to waste. Call in some back up—readers you trust—to break a tie. Sometimes a single reader gets excited about a single piece and can make a case for reconsideration—listen! (I've seen slush pile readers do this to really good effect, being quite specific on *why* a piece is worth attention.) On the more problematic side, an excited slush pile reader contacts the writer, suggesting that the magazine is "interested." Uh oh, now what? (Make sure the job description for a staff reader looking through the slush pile is very clear—remind them at the start of every reading period about the rules of the job.) As slush piles get read and discussions take place, leading (hopefully) to final choices, it's a good idea to have the section editors meet and hear a quick report from each section—you may be surprised at what has come up ("Anyone else notice that we have a lot pieces about birds this time around?") or how one section's experiences with the slush pile can help educate another section.

Another issue that often comes up in general discussions about submitted work: stay on track. Slush pile discussions can wander down an unhelpful road easily. Remember, the staff is volunteering their time. Their time is valuable. One person had a funny thing happen this week, someone else wants to explain why they were late—just keep the meeting moving, focused, and on subject. In most cases the people present in a slush meeting are there because they did the work. While you can plan time for talk and visits before or after the meeting, and make it optional, the section editor has to keep the focus so that the decisions can get done in a timely manner. This is not to say "Hurry up! Rush!" because some problems will take time to figure out. Make sure you have time for that by not wasting time during the meeting on random, unrelated subjects.

At the beginning of each reading period for *The Blue Route,* I remind students: to be open-minded, to appreciate the new and different (the unusual topic, an intriguing juxtaposition of words or images, a striking metaphor), to guard against valuing work because it is familiar to them in terms of content and form, to not immediately dismiss a work because they don't "get it."

—Michael F Cocchiarale, Faculty Advisor,
The Blue Route, Widener University

Finally, have a system for processing your top picks—a folder for definite "yes" files, another for the highest ranked "maybes." You might check these regularly as you move through your considerations for publication. For instance, two pieces might be awfully similar, and very good—which one do you let go? Can you offer one of the writers a spot in the next issue? (Are you the staff for the next issue?) Is a theme shaping up when you look through all the pieces you want to accept? (Is your group tending too much toward only *one* sort of narrative?) Recognize these situations and adjust accordingly. The Editor-in-Chief should be in touch with all the different sections, helping everyone keep their eye on the schedule and the work and the questions.

> Keep discussion moving with POSITIVE criticism. These authors place themselves in an incredibly vulnerable position when they submit their work. Treat every submission as if you are workshopping your peers. Make sure discussion does not veer towards making fun of the author or the work itself. There is a way to provide criticism during production meetings without doing so harshly.
>
> —Carlie Sisco, Editor-in-Chief 2018–2019
> *The Blue Route,* Widener University

Final Decisions on What to Publish

Final decisions on a few of the pieces chosen for publication are easy and happen fast. Everyone loves them. The final-final decisions, however, are the hardest because there is usually … a small problem. Maybe the piece is very good but two readers are quite unfavorable. Perhaps half the slush readers love this piece and the other half love another piece. How "democratic" is your magazine? It's always a question. Do your individual sections decide content, or is the Editor-in-Chief, or the Editor-in-Chief along with managing editors and maybe the section editor calling the final shots together? Try to figure this out ahead and stick to it. (Quick caveat— each method has its pros and cons. You can always have a final nod from the Editor-in-Chief, managing editors, or faculty advisor. While the Advisor might help take some pressure off the students, there are pros and cons to an "outside" choice, too.) And there is always the baseline question, the golden rule of writers and artists: how would you like to see your first publications processed and managed?

The most common problem I've seen with final-final decisions has to do with the presumed (un)acceptability of the material. Is someone going to get mad if we publish this piece? Are there some questionable viewpoints included here, or overdone profanity or violence? At a recent meeting a managing editor asked that we put a trigger warning on a piece of fiction—this was actually during the proofreading process. (The suggestion was voted down; the general consensus included the observation that we had never done this before, though the students decided that a discussion on trigger warnings would happen before the next issue.) If you are unsure about the reception you might get with a certain piece of writing (or art), please please please ask a couple of people outside the organization first, people who know literary publishing. Maybe faculty, maybe graduate students, maybe a community writer. Ask them to explain their thinking, too. (This is crucial—none of you are in a vacuum.) And remember this as well: creative work, artwork, work that is art, is often meant to make us think and consider new ways of seeing. And if you are worried about university administrators, they are often less horrified than you might think. Another camp would say "There is nothing new under the sun" and that might be worth considering too. How expected or worn is the piece under review? Remember, too, that characters are not roommates, ideas are meant to be discussed, and value judgments are personal. Consider ethics (we always do this, even if we think we aren't), and know your own morality. Be very aware, as well as you can, about *why* you are making the decision you are making. Spend time parsing it out. Whatever you do, you will learn something.

Socially, we have some clear rules about language, about stereotyping—and about misogyny and racism, bigotry and fear. For helpful background, see Chimamanda Ngozi Adichie's "The danger of a single story," a TED talk you can find on YouTube.

Space is always an issue when making final-final decisions. Can you fill the pages with the kind of quality material you seek? Is this volume going to be slim, or do you have the funds to make it a bit larger than normal when you have great material? How many amazing poems came through this time? It's not so bad if this issue has more poetry than usual or poetry that's not like the poetry published last time. Do you have space for that very long experimental prose piece on medical-social movements? These discussions should be open and thorough. As much as you plan ahead, there will likely be some questions as you finish up the decision-making process. Remain flexible and know your limits (like time and funding). If you need it, seek counsel.

Our job is to make a great issue, not publish only the very best stuff that comes into our submissions. Some we will miss, and they will get published elsewhere. John Lyons, Drama Editor, *earthwords: the undergraduate literary review*, University of Iowa

Editing for Layout

Student journals often have a quick turnaround time, meaning that between the time you decide you would like to publish a poem or story or artwork or interview and the moment it is ready for layout, well, a lot of things have to happen:

- **Basic editing**—start right away making sure for each piece you want to publish that usage is consistent; check spelling and grammar and spacing and punctuation and missing words, etc. by marking up a copy of the piece that you will send to the writer for review (section editors should work on these edits—if two people confer on an accepted submission in order to finalizing the piece for layout, only one person should be contacting the writer); make sure the piece is solid and that a series of small edits will only improve it. (See Figure 3.1 for basic editing marks.)

- **Ask the writer/artist FIRST: Is the piece still available?** (Has the writer already promised the piece to another publisher?); ask this in writing, so there is a record; "If it is still available, we are interested in publishing it"; this is the most fun part of putting together a magazine, sending that acceptance note and hearing back from a happy writer.

- **Once the writer/artist agrees to have you publish their work, ask the writer/artist to send a bio** (or bio and photo) right away; be very clear on what you are looking for: a 100-word bio? Fifty? a photo in what format/resolution?); you are giving the writer/artist something to do while you complete the copy edits; let them know about the production schedule, the date by which the bio and final edits are going to be due.

- **Edit with your style sheet in hand (see below) and send the marked-up poem/story/essay/interview to the writer/artist along with any questions;** (does your magazine use m dashes with no spaces or spaces with n dashes? etc.); ask if they meant to use italics *here* and not there; ask them about consistency in punctuation; suggest that they re-paragraph in one particular spot because they did so in the same situation everywhere else; how does your magazine format section breaks? Tell the writer. Get your editing questions all lined up before you send the list of them to the writer (see Figure 3.2).

- **Notify the writer/artist that you are available for questions** about the edits (and then follow through by keeping an eye on your inbox); be very clear about deadlines.

- **Never change the text in a way that changes the meaning** without asking the writer first; never *ever* do that; for poets, never assume

GENERAL EDITING MARKS

FIGURE 3.1 *An example of basic editing marks. This is not an exhaustive list, and styles on editing marks vary. Just be consistent.*

that anything, not capital letters or line breaks or anything at all, can be changed without asking first.

- **Ask the writer/artist to keep an eye on their inbox** in case something comes up last minute while layout and proofreading is going on.

- **If a writer does not respond, make sure you try all the contact info you have and then send one last email that clearly states you**

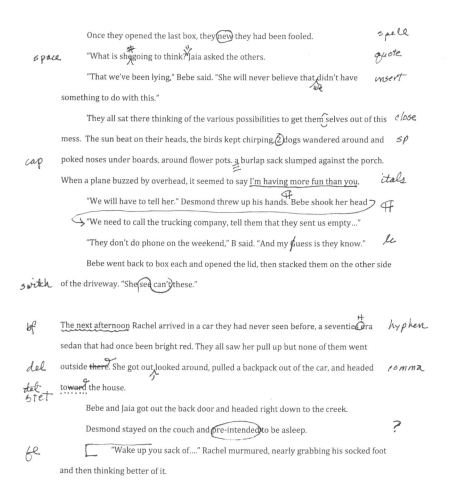

FIGURE 3.2 *A sample manuscript page with examples of editing marks—far too many for one page, of course.*

are moving on (not publishing) if you don't hear by (date/time)— polite and direct; save that email—cc a few people on it and then move on; this is another reason you don't want to send out rejection notes too fast—you may need the piece that was *almost* accepted when a favored piece has been accepted elsewhere or a writer/artist flames out on correspondence.

Keep a file on the web where you collect all the pieces that are ready for layout—meaning the writer has given final approval on the copy you have worked over together. Make sure you talk with your layout person about what they need (spacing requirements, indents) so you can make any

Style Sheets: Remember when you were writing in high school and you had to use an official handbook of grammar and punctuation rules like the MLA Handbook or APA Style? And then you got to college and someone explained that, well, yeah, really there are several rulebooks on usage in English—happens in maybe most languages—and that different institutions and groups have their own style manuals? Your college or university probably has a style guide for the website and their publications. (When do you capitalize Provost and when is provost written in lower case?) Your journal should have one of these, too. Or you should ascribe to one that's already established (AP is commonly used) and if you have some specific differences you want followed (when to use m dashes and when to use n dashes; how headers and footer must appear; a figure for section breaks) then make a list of those for your handbook.

last-minute adjustments *before* the edited pieces go to layout. And don't forget to tell the writers and artists about the launch date—and the number of copies (usually one or two) the writer/artists receive(s) as compensation.

It's unlikely you are paying contributors, but if you are, you will also need to draw up a contract and get it signed before you distribute any money. (Your email thread with the writer suffices for basic publication agreements where money does not change hands and rights revert to the author.) You can find, online, sample publication agreements and discussion of the necessary contract clauses—and see Appendix B.

Sequencing and Proofreading

Once you have collected all the material for your next issue, and the basic copy editing is done, you have a few decisions to make. First, what expectations for this issue does your choice of artwork for the cover or homepage for this issue suggest? This may or may not be a group discussion, and of course your art staff will have something to say—they will likely have, at least, some further suggestions on design (again, be clear on the processes ahead of time so no one is blindsided) for the page surrounding a lead visual. There are a few parameters which are quite simple: the size and resolution of the image; will the image work with the journal's format; is this cover image too much like the last one; are you also including the image inside the journal or on other pages (even in thumbnail, with basic artist information, on the Table of Contents page)? If you are publishing online you don't have to have any "cover" art, but you will have to make layout design decisions based on the art you've chosen. The visual style of your online journal, if you haven't already purchased a template, needs to be respected and perhaps the decisions handled by the art staff together with design staff. (You can always look at what other people have done with their online literary journals and compare. There's a lot to choose from.) Be sure to have your design, graphics, and layout persons present at these conversations so you know what's possible.

Whether you are printing a journal or presenting the work online, sequencing is important because you have to imagine leading the reader/viewer through the experience of your journal. How do you want them to encounter this particular set of artistic works?

For print, it's rather simple, unless you are working with a design that is not a typical book—more on that in a moment. Sequencing is linear, one piece after another, even if everyone doesn't read them that way. Are you going to put all the art together, on nicer paper in the middle of the book or spaced between other pages? (Be in touch with your printer and see what they can do with different papers, folios, and/or text pages versus color pages. When you are on a tight budget they can tell you which papers and formats work the best for both text and color images.) Is all the fiction (poetry, nonfiction) going together in one section, or are you mixing the genres throughout? Do you need a special section for contest winners? Are you doing the standard style of putting the bios of your artists/writers at the back of the book or on the first page of their creative work at the bottom (or top) in small type? How are you setting up the Table of Contents—as a simple list in order, or with all the poetry listed together, the art listed together, etc., no matter where it shows up in the book? Author's names first, or title? The best way to make these decisions is to look at what other journals do and pick the features you like the best. Make sure the chosen elements work together properly, that there are no inherent contradictions.

It's best that you don't reinvent the wheel (the design wheel) each year or with each issue (again, if design is part of your mission, hold on a moment, I'll get to that). If you keep redesigning the journal (or the logo, or the typeface, font, etc.) it will not help with getting some recognition—literally, the journal has to be recognizable to stick in people's minds. You probably want at least some consistent design elements. So if you are inheriting a layout, consider sticking with it and making only minor adjustments of the sort that help send you in the direction you want to go. (And be clear re: how and why.) Take particular care with your font—choose one that is easy on the eyes and does justice to poetry and prose. Don't suddenly print everything in twelve-point font if you've been using ten. If you are starting from scratch, make sure you keep in mind the fact that someone will be working with your files later so make design choices that make sense for future layout persons.

On where to put each piece in a print journal (sequencing), consider also how the different pieces fit together. You don't want a poem about losing a piece of jewelry right after a story about a jewel heist. (Probably you don't want that. Maybe you do.) You could put a drawing of children playing next to a story about losing a child, but ... *hmmm?* The main point here is this: if you are going to use a piece of artwork to "illustrate" (work with) a piece of fiction (or poetry or nonfiction), *or* you want to use a piece of fiction to lend backstory to a piece of artwork, you must (MUST) ask the artist and writer first. Essentially, when you are doing this kind of pairing, you are making meaning out of someone else's work—visual and written. Be reasonable and ask first. If you are simply designing for a general tour through some remarkable works of individual merit, then consider how a piece that is dark but funny might be followed by something that brings the reader to a fresh stance by using unrelated material—then move on to the next dark piece. Maybe something experimental in between? Don't put three pieces on baby birds together ... by accident. Be very mindful of what each piece is and place it so that it gets full attention on equal grounds to all the other pieces of art and writing.

For online journals it's a little different—and a little the same. There are design choices you are probably working with already (the theme or basic design structures of your site) but you have to figure out how to list the works—a similar Table of Contents page with links, a full downloadable PDF of the print file (see previous paragraphs on print sequencing, basically), or links by section, artwork separate or with poems and stories paired, etc. Do you want to feature some of the works in the Table of Contents with bold typeface or tile links? Again, look at the websites of other online journals (there are some listed in Appendix A) and figure out what you want. I've noticed that with a few exceptions online journals are going with a very simple look these days, very spare pages (easy to focus on the text or image), lots of white space, and minimal options for navigation on each page. For the opposite, see *The Rumpus*, which features very busy pages and lots of ads that are probably paying the bills. Again, this is now, and only now—all this will change and keep changing. The point about sequencing and an online journal is basically the same as print: how do you want to lead your reader through the experience of that issue, and how can you make sure that anyone looking at that issue can find, easily, any piece that appears in that issue? You can upload a PDF of an issue on your website, with "pages" to turn, a kind of virtual print journal. There are so many choices, so many ways to go about this, you simply must research some websites and see what you find appealing and easy to access. Your readers will not stick with you if you make navigation confusing or counterintuitive.

Proofreading is another matter, and I have to admit that this is one of my favorite parts of production. Once the layout person has put the journal together (we will talk about layout in a moment) you can print out (or look online at unpublished web pages—ask your web editor) the whole issue and see how it looks and take one last inspection for any extra commas, dashes, italics, dangling modifiers, missing capital letters—and fix them. (The list of potential little corrections is endless. But try.) Make sure your layout person has proofreading marks on every item that needs to be changed, a map for making corrections. Use standard editing marks and use them consistently. Check headers, footers, line spacing, guttering, indents, etc.

I prefer the proofreading method where every section (art, poetry, prose, etc.) takes their own page proofs by section—managing editors perhaps take the bios and front matter—and pour through them for anything amiss. It might be necessary to give the sections a weekend to do a thorough job. Have one person collect all the corrections and mark up one copy for the proofing meeting. Maybe give everyone a few days plus a weekend to read everything, and then everyone meets for an afternoon. The upper staff goes through the whole magazine, together, page by page. All problems are worked out right there—and one person, only one, keeps a master copy of all the final changes for the layout person to go back and correct. (There will be much discussion on a few small points, believe me.) During this process, do not change your mind about basic directions you've already given. Don't frustrate your layout person by changing the rules on commas, for instance. On the other hand, if you need one exception (for a very good reason) take it.

It is vital to assist your layout person by making sure that everyone does their full copyediting job *before* any file goes into the layout folder. You don't want scores of simple mistakes up for discussion at the proofing meeting. If early editing is done well, the proofing meeting is simple and straightforward. You find where the layout might have changed a line break or paragraphing, check that all the page numbers are correct, catch that place where one letter is not italicized, etc. During proofreading, have the layout folder of copyedited pieces there for reference—along with the original piece from the writer nearby. Did the writer add a new section break here? Oh—there are two section breaks in the page proofs, so one has to go. Etc. etc. etc.

This is not the only way to do it, and you can obviously complete your proofreading over several days with editable files, on the web, using Google Docs for instance, but I've also seen people come close to blows when one person thinks they see everything perfectly and starts changing this and that asynchronously—what a mess. Rather, add some pizza and snacks to a long proofing meeting—plus at least one break to get up and stretch. The camaraderie of a smooth (because all the previous work was properly done) proofing meeting is a nice touch, a way for the crew to share their pride in the work. Creating an issue of your magazine is like a group art project. Sitting together for the "making" can raise the level of artistic value of the final product.

Once the final-final edits are entered into layout, there is the final-final proofing: one more close look to be certain that all the corrections are entered and that they look right, haven't caused another issue (lines move around, maybe pages change—you might have to quadruple-check the Table

Many writing teachers will tell you that the rubber meets the road during the revision process, that if you are not good at revision (if you can't "kill your darlings" for the sake of a better final outcome for your story, poem, or drawing) you will never make it as a writer or artist. Before you decide that you are rotten at that sort of thing, work on a literary magazine for a while. See what it's like to edit. Get a taste for what happens to your work when you send it out and someone has to kick it into shape for the page. I'm not saying that magazine edits are huge, I'm just pointing out that you can learn a lot about revision by being an editor for other people. You see the work of the writer/artist from a different angle and it can help you see your own work in a way that is helpful to your own revision practice.

of Contents). This can be done individually or with a smaller number of people. It's the very fine tuning. (See Mary Norris's *Between You and Me* (2015), about exhaustive copy editing at the *New Yorker*.) Other things might come up that you didn't see before. People can get upset about this, about not catching it the second or third time, but it's all polish, and it's very hard to catch everything. With an online journal you can easily fix any errors that, let's say, an author points out after the pages go live, or a staff member, who was not involved in early proofing efforts and who has a good eye for web pages, catches quickly. On web pages you often have to see how something works (links between pieces, scrolling on a long piece) and the web editor will simply have to keep making adjustments and corrections. Not unusual. Just don't let errors stand too long. If writers see that you don't adequately (and beautifully) present the work online, they will not want to submit to your online journal. You want to do justice to the contributors' work and yours.

For print journals, you will be given a printer's proof—essentially a single copy of the actual book that you must check carefully for any errors they might have made, or for things that you want changed. This is an important distinction. If they made errors (pages missing, print not readable, etc.) they have to correct that and send you another printer's proof. If you made the errors (the resolution of photos is not right and the images are blurry; you have guttered the poems—meaning the poems are so far to the right on the left page or so far to the left on the right page that you have to crack the book's spine to read them) then that's *your* mistake and more editing and layout work must be done. This will cost you—both time (the time it takes to correct the problem and get another printer's proof) and money (the money it will cost to make that second printer's proof, which is usually between about $50 and $100 for a simple, perfect-bound book). Again, people might get a little upset, but such corrections are not unusual and if you plan ahead with a little wiggle room for your production process, the worst that can happen is that things go incredibly smoothly and you get your boxes of books well ahead of the launch party.

When all the work is done and the issue is completed and the layout person has done the incredible job of revising and putting up with many voices/ideas, be sure to thank them. Layout is meticulous labor. Everyone on staff should be proud of the work they've done, but the crew on the last stages of this process are the ones that deserve a lot of credit for the visual pleasure, or the tactile pleasure, of the final product.

4

A Few Other Issues Concerning Production

The following are a few other considerations on the design and production of your journal. Some of these can be revisited once you have produced your first issue (not necessarily the first issue of the magazine but the first one you produce) and want to consider some further concerns. Keep a running list, as you move through production, so you can revisit the issues you might not have had time to completely settle.

Design

If you are making an artifact, a book, or designing a web page where you want people to stay and read, you have to think about design. If you are inheriting a journal, design issues might already be decided, more or less—if there's been effort to (re)brand the current journal you might think twice before changing it all up, especially if that's already been done recently.

During Covid, many journals went online and had an opportunity to think seriously about web design in a new way. Perhaps more students will now be interested in learning about web design. There are so many considerations packed into design—including diversity concerns. Are you inviting in an array of readers? Are you highlighting only one type of writer-artist/image with your layout? Be careful of using visuals that seem to represent an easy nod to diversity when what you really need to do is actually seek it, give new individuals power, and forefront the efforts of the many.

Physical books have lasting impact as artifacts. What do you want to illustrate about your moment? At minimum you of course have choices on paper and fonts (and size and color and layout and images). Think about design ahead of time, not when you are in the thick of production. Consider finding artists whose work you would like to define the issue. Talk to art historians at your institution—or librarians—and perhaps find a little-known bit of history about the visual arts (or specific artist from the past) in your area. Look around when you have time to research your options. That research should include talking to printers and web designers you are likely to use and getting their ideas on the best and most economic options for something better and interesting—different, even. Consider the inks the printer uses. Make your own covers with recycled materials. A design shift might include hiring a web designer for your student journal (an output that may serve for many years) or getting in touch with your business college for marketing ideas. They might have an information/communication business technology program, classes that take on projects, or active students who would volunteer to take on your website.

Think critically and wisely. Do not be lured into design ideas by shopping websites that advertise great sales advantage to their layout, or even author websites, because those have a very different purpose. Look for websites that do what you are going to do: publish many people over time with clear and easy access to all the important parts of your total activities plus archiving—add to that the readability for longer texts and/or reasonable visual placement of a poem or audio/video file on a page.

Maybe you are aware of the student journal awards that AWP confers annually, The National Program Directors Prize (https://www.awpwriter.org/contests/national_program_directors_prize_overview). There are two prizes, really: one on content and one on design. Your student journal can apply to these awards at no cost to you. The winners are usually announced at the annual AWP conference. General information is listed along with links to the guidelines. The prize is $1000 for each category and online journals are welcome to apply. The deadline has been in March for the past few years and students can now submit their own journals (it used to be that the faculty advisor had to nominate).

Design is a constant question for literary magazines that change leadership so often, as a student journal does. That's one problem—turnover. Everyone has an opinion—so you should have plenty of ideas. Of course new staff has to orient themselves toward so many new activities and pressures, it can be hard to spend the extra time considering design features. But if you have a strong art team that works well with the graphics section and web editor—plus there is a desire and some resources (the money to pay a designer or the connection to a graduate student in design)—it could be worthwhile to up the artistic quality of your journal.

Think of *McSweeney's*, which for years put out each issue as an art book. One issue was published in a stack of foldouts that went in a rather typical, old-fashioned book box, another looked like a pile of junk mail, on and on, never the same. Subscriptions for a year are rather exorbitant, as one could easily understand re: production costs. You don't have to go that far, but you could do something creative every once in a while. Think outside the book or web page. It's rather fun—and you can do it while also keeping the journal's purpose and reputation in mind.

Printers   *book mobile local*

Most student print journals have to send their magazine files outside the university for printing, while a few have in-house university print shops (you are more likely to have this at a large urban public university or a private university with some history and a lot of endowments). If your journal is also a registered student journal or paid for by your department or college, you might have rules that say you must get three (let's say) bids for the print job before you choose which printer. So you have to find several printers. One of those could be the university printer. There are probably some local or regional printers of perfect-bound books (your most likely print format). You can also get a pretty fast quote from a nationally known printer of literary journals like Sheridan (https://www.sheridan.com/) or Bookmobile or Thomson-Shore (e-book services available here too) who also do fulfillment (sending out your journal to subscribers). There are fewer printers around these days, for obvious reasons—we simply don't need to spend that kind of resources disseminating information on paper. Okay, electricity isn't free either—and screen time has been a drain on most of us in the pandemic—but most students are aware of the need to use less paper. Everyone needs to balance their use of natural and sustainable resources. For more info on the printing process and printing terms, check out this page on the website for the Council of Literary Magazine Publishers (CLMP) website: https://www. clmp.org/wp-content/uploads/2016/04/intern_training_manual.pdf

Here's the reason I'm including a separate section on this subject: books can be beautiful and printers are underutilized. Printing has changed in recent years. There are recycled papers, technologies that make printing streamlined and cheaper, plus inks that are not so environmentally horrible. (Imagine putting together an issue with plant-based disappearing ink! But I digress.) I'm not suggesting that everyone do this, but I am suggesting that if you are devoted to print, you can perhaps work on your design by working with your printer. Ahead of time, of course. They know what they are capable of doing and they also want to make something beautiful. When printers know that you are a student journal, working with limited resources and for educational purposes, some will (I hate to say) run in the other direction or perhaps deign to answer your calls with a chill pause, but others will be thrilled to help you out and will assist with making something gorgeous. The partnership takes time and attention. An ongoing partnership is precious.

Also, if you are in a rural area or a small town far from a large enough city, you will probably have to hire a printer that is not within range for the type of face-to-face business dealings that printing consultations require. A printer's proof will have to be mailed to you and you will have to have your books shipped when the job is complete. All that takes time, and money, but, again, the effort to set something up that can be reproduced might be worth it. When you are doing your research and you come across a beautiful journal, consider contacting that journal and asking who their printer is. You can ask other student literary journals (perhaps through FUSE) who they use. Some journals go as far as other continents for their printing, and I don't suggest that simply because the wait-time is too long for the schedule of an undergraduate magazine and that kind of shipping is not environmentally friendly either. Again, research, connections and planning will help.

Soliciting Submissions

Should you ask specific people to submit work to your journal? Like a famous writer you admire who is visiting your university or college? As I've mentioned, think twice about that. The work that "famous writer" is willing to have you print is maybe not their best, but you asked for it, and now what do you do? You could ask for other work, some more choices, but that sounds a little ungrateful. As mentioned earlier, consider asking the famous writer you encounter (at your school, at a conference, at a reading) for an interview that you can put in your journal or on your website. Work out the questions carefully so that you don't ask the kind of question that any writer would answer the same way. ("Yes, it was hard to get started because I didn't know the industry.") Really read the writer's work and figure out an angle on the questions that would actually be interesting to the people who read that writer and your particular journal. Keep the thread of questions on target, and be very thorough with formatting your interview in print, sending your text to the writer for edits, making changes and getting a final okay from the writer for the version you want to print (this is vital—get a final okay and change nothing after that). Send a separate thank-you note on letterhead and a copy of the journal (or link) once it is published.

Another situation: you may be in a writing class and come across some student work that's really outstanding. Take the time to ask that writer to submit to the journal and be ready with all the relevant information. Or send an email with the appropriate links. If it happens that a number of editors are attending a reading together and the section editor is there too (the poetry editor for a piece of poetry, let's say), put your heads together and decide if you want to offer the writer a spot for that piece, right now. You can always suggest that if the piece is not available, you would "like to look at other work, if you are interested in our journal." Always have some attractive bookmarks or cards you can carry with you that have the website and email listed. Then be sure to follow up, to pay attention, to not drop the ball. Choose your language carefully and do not promise what you cannot keep. Writers remember these moments, appreciate them, and will remember you.

Cold calling requests for work (just writing someone and asking them to send their work) can sound like you are promising to publish. And that's dicey, for the reason stated twice already. If you have prior experience with a respected writer, and you know you can be direct about the "fit" of whatever they send, that's different, go ahead. But just know that a solicitation is not a ho-hum thing and should not be offered lightly.

Awards or Not

A writing contest sounds fun because we seem to be a culture that loves a competition. I am not a fan of competitions or awards. At an undergrad literary magazine which does not have endless funding, it seems to me that the money could be better spent to the benefit of more people. Not a bad idea, a discussion of what "benefit" means, especially if there is no easy agreement on the definition and your staff can listen to each other on the subject of awards. Honestly, awards do get people's attention (they are a type of advertising), and it's hard to measure the pros and cons of that kind of recognition.

The first question is this: an award for what? The usual answer is fiction, poetry, or nonfiction (or journalism or short form or genre, etc.). You can mess with the categories. Any creative writing of only one page? The best villanelle? Tiny artwork? You get the picture. The next question is the award—what can you afford or what can you get someone to donate for the award? (This is a good way of getting a donation—putting someone's name on the award, or attracting a donor who may want to honor someone.) The larger the cash award the better—well, the more submissions you might get. Are you trying to make money with this award, collecting submission fees? Lots of journals live off that model. Designing the award means targeting an audience, too: your department, your college, your university, or your town, state, region, country—or a particular sort of writer/writing. You have to figure out what is appropriate for the situation or the parameters you are handed—by the donor, your department, school, whatever.

For instance, a few years ago when I went to ask the provost at our university for a donation to the undergraduate literary magazine, she invited a non-academic VP to the meeting who suggested that we take the opportunity to highlight the creative writing program and include the whole university—and put a positive spin on the Provost's Office. The award was significant ($2500 in fall for prose, and $2500 in spring for poetry), open to all undergrads who were registered at the school (even part time), and the winners were published in the alumni magazine. The readers were graduate students at the creative writing program, the final judges the creative writing faculty. No names were allowed on the entries—student ID numbers only. Before the finalists were sent to the faculty judges, we had to check the registration status of each student's entry. We had an advisor do this part— we never matched names and IDs until the end, when the faculty judges came back with a winner. The award seemed popular. Students often said that an award of that amount would make their lives easier. One person got to pay a few bills. The publication part made better sense to me: the audience for this award would be former students of the university, students who worked in a vast array of professional careers.

Here are some basics about contests:

- **Do not start an award without having a thorough plan.** You need some lead time to set it all up and get everyone on board.

- **Write up the guidelines.** "The theme is *joy*," "Up to ten pages of prose," "Only one submission per person," "If the piece is accepted for publication elsewhere, the writer must inform the magazine by the end of the semester," "Each submission requires a three-dollar processing fee," "To be eligible you must be a resident of Arkansas," and etc. You choose. Set out the guidelines for the manuscript, as well: "1 inch margins, sans serif font, the title centered and ID # in the upper right of each page, clearly marked section/stanza breaks, writer's name appearing exactly nowhere on the manuscript"; you can also throw out the submissions that do not follow the guidelines—this can be a hard lesson, but a worthwhile one for most writers (and editors!).

- **Have a clear submission deadline** which takes account of all the necessary facts—time for judging to be completed (you need weeks)—in line with whatever the prize may be (your publishing schedule, a registration to your annual conference, etc.); you will also need a clear deadline for the judging process; let your judges know when they need to have the scoring completed; be clear (to yourself at least) that if you say all submissions are read by two people, you have done the math and such a promise can be kept.

- **Line up your judges ahead;** let them know what they are being asked to do. "We are asking each initial judge to read and score ten manuscripts of not more than ten pages each—if you can read more than one ten-entry packet, we will arrange that"; if there is payment involved, be clear that payment only happens when the work is done; graduate students can put a line on their CV for judging and faculty can use the fact of their helping out at their annual review (helping in this way is called "service"); thank everyone multiple times—when they say "sign me up," when you send them the materials, and when they finish the work; always tell writers who the judges are—in the call for submissions, if possible.

- **How do you want the judges to judge?** You can have them meet and talk it out, you can set up a score sheet (with some guidelines, of course, like "5 is the highest praise a submission can get and 1 is the lowest" and then you add these up and move the highest five or ten entries to the next level); do not add, in the judges' directions, "quality" guidelines than the writers did not get; tell judges the same thing you told the writers and no more because it is unfair and a waste of time if you add another hurdle after the fact; for this reason, be very careful about who you ask to judge; ask someone who can adequately judge the sort of writing you asked for.
- **Be clear about where the award will be announced and when.** "By the end of fall semester we will post the winner on our website."
- **Never post a winner until you speak with them**—and, again, ask the writer to confirm that the piece was not published elsewhere, that it is still available for publication; ask if you might use excerpts later on the website; offer to answer their questions about the award; before going live with a winner, some places even run their entries through Turnitin.com.
- **Let your judges know who the winner is ahead of time**—or let them know they can check the website by such-and-such a date; thank them, again, for choosing this marvelous gem.
- **Make sure the prize (publication, money, a ticket to travel to X) is delivered in a timely fashion**; no putting it off.
- **Consider a list of Honorable Mentions** or second place, third place, etc. A group of Honorable Mentions is more egalitarian.
- **Advertise:** just like you had a plan to advertise the contest, have a plan to advertise the winner (same thing—email, social media, homepage, etc.); if it's an annual award, have a list of past winners available somewhere on your website.

There are plenty of other types of awards that colleges and universities provide to students. If you are a registered student organization, for instance, there may be leadership awards (let the people who can nominate you know that you are interested), or there may be publication awards that include a university newspaper and other publishing concerns run by students. You might want to have a set of awards at the end of the year for your staff or an award chosen by your staff (Section Editor of the Year or Best Fiction for 2020–2021). Maybe a local bookstore would donate a gift card. Your department might have writing awards for creative writing and your staff—after a long year of classes and editing other people's work—can submit and get their creative work recognized. There may be a university award for recognition of support for intellectual engagement in the university community. Don't be shy—get your organization or the membership/staff out there in front.

There may also be state or local awards where you can submit your publication for content or design awards. Most states hold a book festival at the state capitol once a year—do a little research and see if there is something you can apply to for recognition of your work and the journal's final product.

The Lonesome Job of the Editor-in-Chief

Being the Editor-in-Chief is exhausting, and difficult, and incredibly rewarding. Not many people want to take it on. The best applicants come from the ranks of the literary magazine—students who have seen how the organization works and have maybe been readers, section editors, and perhaps even managing editor. Their ideas for change might have a basis in experience—wonderful! This is not to say that a completely new person cannot do the job; I once worked with an Editor-in-Chief who had been the editor of a newspaper at her high school, nothing else at the college level—and she did a great job. There are numerous personality traits that can help: leadership skills; being able to attract people who want to work with you; organizational acumen (having a knack for the automatic, economical flow chart in your head—as well as patience with painstaking detail); a sense of humor (no one likes a grumpy boss); enthusiasm (vital for any nonprofit work); healthy self-esteem (not egotistical, neither a pushover); an ability to be humble (thank people who help and recognize those who have good ideas); and basic dependability (if you say you will do something, you do it).

There can be some really bad fails, too: editors who come to meetings drunk, who talk rudely to staff and have a hard time giving credit when credit is due (no one works in a vacuum at a literary magazine or at any nonprofit). People who pick fights, can't get along, or can't get out of their own way, or expect full agreement all the time—no one wants to work with that. As an advisor who has to choose (when we do summer interviews for staff for the upcoming year), I find that if an applicant (anyone) comes with a list of things they will not do, that's an easy "No thank you" for me. Unfortunately, I have had to say goodbye to a number of people over the years who *should* have been able to take on the leadership job they applied for. However, I would not put someone in a position of power who had already shown that they would abuse that power or not wield it with some self-awareness of their presence—whether they saw it that way or not. In some cases, applicants who felt they had been treated unfairly by someone else on staff were actually right. But the way they handled themselves in that situation told me everything I needed to know about what would happen next. If I let someone go, I tried to speak with the applicant to let them know that I saw their potential, absolutely, but in this case (often a very hard decision—other times less difficult) there was a distinct problem which led me the other way.

People working two jobs, living with roommates or family, who have health issues, who are taking classes full time—and maybe all of these things at once—have been incredibly successful at the top job. Success is more about allowing involvement. The best Editor-in-Chief is someone who can feel part of the group and also separate from it without freaking out. They can confidently delegate. They can agree to disagree. They will make mistakes and ask for help. There are times when the one at the top will not be thanked, will be blamed, will be blameworthy or innocent, will wish they had done or said something different—the list is endless. An Editor-in-Chief can easily have a raging fit—as long as they work on the problem (their part) and come to a new understanding. The best thing about encountering all this personality stuff in a workplace environment is that the undergraduate literary magazine happens to be a great place to develop and adjust one's workplace behavior and ethics. I have seen many Editors-in-Chief (and section editors) have a tough time, keep the train on the tracks, and go on to do confident work with generosity and skill.

Leadership is an opportunity to get to know yourself. Every Editor-in-Chief I've ever worked with has had the problem of not being listened to at certain moments, for instance. Frustrating! Well, guess what? No one is paid (well, mostly no one is paid—if they do get a stipend, they better listen up). There are times when everyone is tired and no one wants to hear that something didn't get done or that this one thing must be done a certain way so the layout person doesn't go nuts: everyone says "Yeah, sure, you bet!" and then does the same unhelpful thing again. And again. A good Editor-in-Chief does her/his/their best to call the next move and to learn from what happens.

Hear me out: it is so easy in a tough situation to say "Hey, it's not personal" because it really isn't—everyone has their burden to bear and you cannot even begin to guess how one person came about the ability (or the lack of ability) to be reasonable. As the leader, you have to keep going, even when you are tempted to say something. Over and over again I have said to an upper editor who is fuming (or in tears), "Don't give that person the power to derail you. No matter what they said or did, you have power *only*

Trust yourself. You are in this position, however it came to be, because someone trusted that you have the ability to do it well. Literary magazines have innumerable moving parts, and it can be easy to get stuck in a loop of decision-making, questioning, doubling back, and doubting yourself. Instead, trust yourself to make a decision and make it well. This will save both you and your team headaches and unnecessary stress, and the finished product will be all the better for it.
                                        —Melinda Mayden, Editor-in-Chief,
                                        Glass Mountain Magazine, 2019–2020

over your reaction. Don't give them that power—keep it for yourself. You will need the energy." At the same time, I have to admit that I was in my thirties before I was able to do that myself—after being told the same thing over and over by people around me. It's a hard lesson. When a section editor recently spoke during a meeting about a revenge poem she had written about a breakup—she wanted to send it to the person who had broken her heart—our Graduate Advisor wisely said "Don't give that person the gift of your wonderful poetry. They no longer deserve your artistic attention." Well said.

My final point is that during interviews for the position of Editor-in-Chief, I always bring up this one point: the Editor-in-Chief has a lonesome job. At some point you are likely to piss off everyone—even when you try not to. You've got to weather the storm. You can't be nice and be happy all the time, every minute. When an Editor-in-Chief many years ago overruled the entire art staff and chose the cover art herself, I tried to unruffle some feathers because she'd made an excellent choice—but I heard about it for years after. (I still think she made a good decision.) When you lead, and you want to be as democratic and transparent as possible—which is an excellent idea and I highly suggest you do that as a fundamental principle—there will still be moments when things don't exactly look right. And you will have to

The editorial team I worked with was passionate about representation and diversity. It was embedded in all of their decisions and they were devoted to bringing it into the bones of the organization and magazine. Some of their staff, however, were not as devoted. Toward the end of the academic year tensions began to run high and the editorial team felt that one staff member was overstepping his bounds and not being cognizant of the organization's devotion to diversity. As a white woman in the role of the graduate advisor I didn't know how to help the upper editors, both women of color, manage this tension with their white male staff member. Were they made to feel comfortable as women of color in positions of power at our institution? I am middle class and have often benefited from a middle-of-the-road stance. I admired their steadfastness. Tension, however, bled into other relationships and very few editors and staff ended the year happy. Try as we might, faculty and advisors cannot always create a level playing field for all our students. There may be an unequal understanding of the playing field itself. When students are engaging in questions of equality and diversity they often think about the pages of the magazine they are working with and may forget the people they are working with.

—Josephine Mitchell, Graduate Advisor,
Glass Mountain Magazine, 2017–2018

sit with that appearance, knowing that you did the best you could for the best reasons possible. Be kind to yourself.

Recruitment

While four years of higher ed might seem like a long time, it goes fast—once you have completed core classes and entered a major, the last years of study may be the perfect time to try out a professional activity you can put on your resumé. Again, I've been told by job recruiters that even a minor in English can put a job candidate at the top of a ranked list of interviewees because it is expected that this person will know how to read and write with a bit more expertise—quite valuable to most employers. Depending on the structure of your organization and home department, you may need a brand new crew of upper editors every year. This is not usual for most undergraduate literary magazines. You just need to do some recruiting or aim at having a regular rotation. That could mean an agreed-upon two-year commitment. Convincing students that they will have the time to devote to an editing position means being honest about the workload. Many students have families and/or other jobs, so being able to manage time commitments is a real issue. Students have to get something out of the experience— professionally and/or personally. Some students *think* they can do it, but are forced by circumstance (or other interests or commitments) to leave. You have to be ready to support each other and perhaps have other structures (like job sharing) to make up the difference.

Each year you will probably be recruiting some new upper staff members, new readers for sections, new section leaders (what I'm calling "upper editors") and probably a leader, an Editor-in-Chief (the longest serving Editor-in-Chief at the undergraduate level I've worked with is three years— really remarkable). The best situation, again, is when the upper editors have moved through the ranks to that leadership position. Starting as a slush pile reader is not uncommon. Someone who knows how the operation works from a few different angles is probably going to be a better fit for leadership— as long as there isn't some personal agenda in that power position that goes against the organization's needs. (It happens.) This is not to say, as well, that a leadership position cannot be filled by someone with less experience (or no experience) within the organization. If there happens to be no obvious person in line (for section editor, managing editor, or for Editor-in-Chief) the application/interview process can be especially important. Not because the hiring process is airtight, but because the most unobvious thing on paper can show up in an interview and then the choice becomes clear—or clear enough that the risk is worth the unusual choice. I have seen several editors succeed marvelously who came with less editing experience but plenty of leadership experience (for instance with Greek leadership or the mother of twelve children and owner of a goat farm). Listen carefully and ask a lot of questions that will help your applicant describe skills they have that might not have been included in the application.

The first thing to consider on general recruitment is that recruitment happens all the time—when a student gets published by the magazine or reads it and finds it interesting, when the magazine shows up at an event, or when a professor mentions the organization in a creative writing class. (As mentioned here elsewhere, reading and editing for a magazine is a marvelous way of moving your own craft forward, as you see how your work might be processed, how decisions are made and how the actual editing comes into play.) Your reputation is your first recruitment tool. Getting someone to fill out an application? Often the current staff will have to reach out numerous times to potential applicants. (Marketing students have pointed out it takes seven "touches" to get the average person to respond.) Be sure to post a message on your website: "Interested in becoming a staff member? Write to us at aaa@bbb.ccc." Keeping your staff application posted to your website 24/7, downloadable and with clear qualifications and directions for submitting, helps a great deal too. Your staff page is probably a good place for a link to the application form. There is a sample staff application in Appendix B.

As mentioned elsewhere in this book, having your current staff visit creative writing classes at the end of the semester (or the beginning) works well to recruit new staff—armed with a few paper application forms, of course, so students can see what the questions are; they can keep the paper copy as a reminder, even if the actual application is submitted online. Holding an informational meeting along with an open mic is another possibility. An email blast (or two) from the organization or your home department usually helps. And asking your staff to invite friends who are interested in writing poetry or fiction, or who are avid readers, works well too.

A regular and agreed-upon application/interview process is necessary (this can go in your handbook), for fairness and continuity. The same goes with

We used to struggle with losing our best editors to graduation each May and rebuilding key positions. Now we stagger the class levels of managing and genre editors, always pairing a veteran editor and a newcomer, thereby ensuring continuity. Community building is also key to retaining staff. Simple things like silk-screening the magazine's new T-shirt (using a student-created design) in the production office and providing free pizza and soda to the always-hungry students goes a long way to making the magazine a site of creativity and community. Encouraging the staff to bring friends to events like T-shirt night is a great recruitment tool.
—Mark O'Connor, Faculty Advisor, *Slab Lit Mag*,
Slippery Rock University

an interview and a discussion between several editors about each applicant. Try to have at least two people in on every interview, and while you spend some time describing what the organization does and what you need, be sure to give the applicant time to answer questions, ask questions, and talk about their interest. You may find out that the person would actually fit in the organization somewhere they didn't even know existed. If you let everyone know what you are looking for first (like in an email) that forethought can focus your process. Be careful of being too prescriptive, however, as some people may think they don't have what it takes when they actually do and can easily learn the other stuff with a bit of direction.

For upper editors and the Editor-in-Chief, it can be a good idea to have a panel of interviewers, to get a wider view of the applicant. Invite the department chair, the outgoing graduate advisor, certainly the faculty advisor (always—they have to work together), and a number of staff from all levels. At least some combination of these. Have questions ready. In some cases, when a decision is tough, send the resumé and application letter (always ask for an application letter where the applicant explains their interest and leadership style for an upper editor position) to your board members (or the department chair, creative writing director, or someone with some knowledge and investment in the organization but not someone who knows the candidates) to take a look and give their considered opinion on the application materials to the interviewing panel. This works best with someone who has done some hiring in the past and has experience with reading between the lines. I cannot tell you how useful another set of eyes can be in this situation.

Once you have new staff, get them in touch with the other staff members they will be working with as soon as possible. Try to arrange access to the people they are replacing—for quick questions. In addition, let your mid-range network know (your department, for example) when you have chosen a new slate of upper editors for the coming academic year—name names and be sure to thank the members of the outgoing staff. Looking forward, try to establish a firm date, far in advance so everyone can put it on their calendars, for a meeting of all the new staff (including returning staff for at least part of the meeting) so you can go over highlights of the coming year, basic policies, new changes in processes, or to get some feedback on outstanding questions. This is also a good time to have breakouts groups, by section, and get everyone introduced to each other and the expectations for future work and slush/editing/proofreading meetings. Take some photos, too—posting photos on your website's staff page is a nice touch.

Themed Issues

The idea of an issue related to a theme comes up all the time—particularly in the present climate. Literally, the climate—floods, hurricanes, fires. Then there's the related pandemics, social movements, and subjects like mental health or addiction recovery. There are more local and specific themes that come up too, of course (rodeos and football riots). All of these have compelled the staff of literary magazines to ask for submissions on a particular topic or idea or abstract concept. It sounds great—even exciting, almost like putting on a show. But the basic question usually comes down to one thing: "Can we get enough submissions on X to reasonably choose from?" Will enough people from the pool of available and likely writers be able to connect to the topic in ways that are both solid and surprising, deep and sure?

If you can gather a big enough pool of submissions, why not try? Be clear on your website and on your submission manager when you write guidelines for this themed issue. If the subject is abstract, give some examples, perhaps. (You WILL be surprised by some of what you get, by certain creative interpretations.) Include a statement, maybe, that explains why you chose this topic or why your readers might be interested in reading about this subject. You can always publish only a few pieces on the theme, or section off the themed part (or publish this topic on your website if you are a print journal; perhaps produce a chapbook if you do web publishing). Some literary magazines do themes as a matter of regular operating procedure: they advertise ahead with a list of the upcoming themes so writers can appropriately submit their work at the right time. Still, a theme will narrow your pool of submissions. And once you start reading, from the editing end, you may see that there are some interpretations which wear you out fast. ("A third of these are about finding a dead bird in the house—who knew that happened so often?") Bottom line, you need a lot of lead time for a themed issue. Plan at least a year ahead. Think about places that you might advertise where you hadn't before but where the ad would be appropriate (even a poster at a bus stop). Consider paid advertising online (with New Pages or *Poets and Writers*) or in a print issue of the *Writer's Chronicle* or Community of Literary Magazines and Presses (CLMP https://www.clmp.org/) if it makes sense. Try posting your submission call in places that might connect with your topic (coffee shops, for a coffee issue) or use hashtags on the subject in Twitter postings.

Quick warning: there will always be that moment in the slush meetings where a really good piece does not get chosen because you really can't quite see how it connects to the theme. There will be people to argue for and against a piece (and people who throw up their hands and say "Now, why did we decide to do a themed issue?") but you can always accept the wonderful piece that is not connected to the themed issue and publish it later. If you accept a piece and the writer agrees to have you publish it later—perhaps when you will NOT be the editor anymore—be sure to have a very clear agreement with the advisor and the next editing crew. It is beyond unfair to accept a piece of writing for a future issue of your magazine if the magazine doesn't publish it.

If you are putting together a print edition of the themed issue, or a PDF accessible online, then the inevitable sequencing of a themed issue is a special case as well. Make sure the placement of text, or texts and art, does not seem to stand as an editorial comment on one piece or the other (see "Sequencing and Proofreading" in Chapter 3).

There is one other instance of the themed issue: the regular issue that seems to fit a theme once all the art and writing has been accepted. Think about that—because it happens. Maybe there's a subject (or subtext) in the air. If you have a large staff reading the slush pile, it is less likely to happen, but it can anyway. If you have a small staff it certainly can happen, and you should think a bit about that and maybe consider your editing process. No matter how it comes about, I've seen the Editor-in-Chief address the matter in the issue's opening letter. That letter, or intro, should also be carefully edited.

Writing the Introduction or "Letter from the Editor" and/or a Dedication

Many magazines have a short, one-page introduction from the Editor-in-Chief to the readers at the opening pages of the magazine. The point is for the Editor-in-Chief to introduce the choices of literary and artistic work included in the issue to the readers and to perhaps give a look behind the scenes at what came up during the editing process—and to thank anyone who helped as well as praise the writers and artists who are "included here."

Such letters are a lovely way to contextualize the issue at hand. Be sure not to air any organizational complaints in such letters, or neglect to recognize someone that deserves recognition. This can be tricky. I've never met an Editor-in-Chief who did not stress over this opening letter. "Did I forget someone? Maybe I should have said that differently," etc. Pass the letter around a bit, to trusted colleagues, for feedback.

The letter also might work with a dedication page. Not everyone includes a dedication with every issue, but it is a regular feature in many literary journals. Students can have some fun with the dedication when it is chosen by the group. There are usually some hilarious suggestions ("Let's dedicate this to everyone affected by Covid") as well as quite somber suggestions, such as a dedication to a student who has recently died. If the dedication is to "Our community of student writers" and the Editor-in-Chief also addresses her/his/their Letter to the same group, that can work well too. Perhaps there were recent changes at the journal that need to be addressed, or a perspective by the upper editors on a recent social movement that can be discussed in a letter from all the upper editors together. Just remember that especially with a print journal, once you write these things down, they remain in the record. If they are posted online, they can spread fast. Be smart, be generous, and always compassionate. Your position of power requires that degree of thoughtful action.

5

Writer Editor Citizen

Writers learning their craft need a community. Editors—whose work is invisible to many—make that community possible. Almost everyone who writes is also an editor of some ilk, but many people have careers in editing i.e., all editors are not equal. Undergraduate literary journals and their home departments typically support a wide range of literary activities: book clubs, study groups, slam performance ensembles. A literary journal legitimizes activities through its connection to the institution and by focusing on the working and social side of literary endeavors—and by inviting the community to come along and have some fun. Reading is a solitary activity. Just like writing, editing is often private and active. Resulting texts have to be shared (published) and celebrated through acknowledgment of all the effort that has gone into the making. As an editor you are going to work behind the scenes and yet be in the spotlight too. You have to create, and manage, the stage.

As mentioned earlier it is quite possible that as an editor at a journal you are also a writer. Undergraduates studying literature and/or creative writing can obviously gain a lot, in terms of their writing lives, by spending some time as literary magazine editors. Knowing how manuscripts are processed before a reader ever sees the publication can help writers (and readers) understand that what they see as "text" has been vetted and processed in a particular manner. Being an editor, you come to understand that "audience" means editor(s) first—and only later does it mean the reader citizen. Put all these positions and activities together and it is called *literary citizenship*.

The word "citizen" in its base form refers to cities—people were once counted as belonging to cities not countries. (A thousand years ago, apparently, there were many more and smaller "countries"—often focused around a central population center.) People in closer quarters have to get along in order to survive and thrive, so cities often provided citizens with a very specific lens from which to see the world—each lens being specific to that region and the needs of the people or rulers, more or less. When we talk about a "literary citizen" we are often speaking about people with a certain ethics and experience around languages and words. Again, not always the exact same morals, but a general interest in the rules re: how words are used and what those rules are and why. "Literary citizen" indicates people who are educated (either within an institution or on their own) in literary matters: they have read many writers, read texts carefully and with curiosity, have had experience with texts on craft, theory, and/or criticism, and might even be writers as well. But not always. The pillars of literary citizenship are often editors—bringing the words of other people to the literary stage. (So many kinds of editors—both in personality and in purpose; even the person you live with, who might read everything you write before you send it out, is an editor, right?)

Other people are reader citizens, by which I mean people that keep open a larger conversation about what texts mean in the social sphere and how they function in the social space. Some readers are not writers. Reading isn't always a critical activity (though some might argue that it is or should be). There are avid readers (of poetry, fiction, nonfiction or all three—go ahead and blur those lines, please!) as well as the book clubs of like-minded readers who use issues of common interest as a lens for reading and discussion, plus those in academia who research the work of one writer (or one concept or period in time, etc.) in order for us all to understand the history of human meaning in words. A "citizen" in the sense I'm using it is an informed member of a group who gets their information through words and observation, maintaining a reflective lens *and* curiosity as a habit—plus a penchant for service to the group.

When we talk about good literary citizenship, then, we are also talking about how we each contribute to the literary efforts in our sphere. Book clubs, bookstores, readings, writing courses, writing conferences—they all put readers and writers (and editors) together. In this section, we will discuss the larger project of connecting your work as a writer, an editor, a reader, and a citizen, to the community around you through events and activities. As an editor it is your responsibility to connect what you do with the people in the literary sphere—in your "city," literal or virtual.

Reading Series and Other Events

To get your magazine some recognition, you have to make some noise, invite people in, and join others in their efforts to focus attention on the readers, writers, educators, and publishers in your realm. By the way, what is your realm? Why does your work as an editor deserve recognition? Go back to the start of this book and recall that you defined yourself, your magazine, in a specific way. Now that you are creating what you set out to make, you have to present your work to the community you designed it for and take note of the reactions in order to gauge the success and do even better next time. In order to promote the work you do, you don't have to do anything terribly flashy, but you do have to be welcoming, aware, confident, and inclusive. (And self-reflective—how did it work? Do people see your efforts the same way you do? Why or why not?) This requires you to reach back into the recent past and recall who you were doing this work for and what your magazine represents. And it requires you to imagine what outreach can look like in your virtual or face-to-face community—and to plan ahead.

Creativity and planning are essential, of course. I've mentioned this so many times I'm sure you are ready to throw the eReader across the room. But let's stop for a minute and focus on the idea of *confidence* in relation to planning. First, no party-planner, ever, has avoided fear of failure, even when they knew they did everything possible to make the magic happen. When start time arrives—the first (or twelfth) time you host an event or join someone else's—and only half the audience you expected has arrived, the show must go on. Please understand that confidence is not braggadocio or simply those behind-the-scenes organizational skills. It's all of it: having an MC that can connect with the audience and readers; making sure the staffers at your merch table know the prices of the merchandise and can speak with knowledge about what the journal does and who you published this time around; it's looking around and embracing what you have, right there at this time in this place, this event, and making it work for everyone involved; it's having fun and making the people involved (including the magazine staff, no matter how new or practiced) feel valued. Do not underestimate the value of confidence in what you do and who you are. (And, always, if you hold events at a restaurant or bar, remind the audience to tip the servers.) Confidence means awareness. It is work that is self-aware.

Now, the events: reading, launch party, open mic, slam, performance, book fair, panel, class, or conference? Each one is a little different and requires you to imagine what would work best *with the other people involved*, meaning staff, readers, the venue, fellow presenters, writers, even the physical space. Where is the table for your magazine going to be at the book fair? Ask for a map. Make sure your readers have water and that the stage is accessible. Don't forget to bring a cash box with plenty of change, a pad of paper receipts, and a credit card reader. How many other people are speaking? How much time does each speaker/reader have? This is your creativity moment, as well as where planning and organizational skills become vital. Plus, you can't do it alone, so event planning is where your most trusted and dependable staff will shine. You have to delegate and communicate.

A final note on the metaphorical city aspect of recent readings and other events, an important new facet: indigenous land acknowledgments. This requires some investigation on your part—to get the details straight. The enactment of such acknowledgments is long overdue, but we do hear them more frequently. You might ask your faculty advisor to find out what has already been researched by other university entities on this topic—or you can simply reach out to the local tribal office and get the information you need. There are also online resources to help you build a solid acknowledgment statement: https://nativegov.org/a-guide-to-indigenous-land-acknowledgment/.

Readings

Many literary magazines host a regular reading series—at the university, local coffeehouses, restaurants, libraries, museums, or bookstores. An old-fashioned used bookstore is a great place for a student-oriented reading because they are the definition of less expensive books. Online readings work very well, especially if there is a moderator who can interview the reader afterward and take questions from the audience. A Zoom license is not very expensive. Online readings can bring in much larger crowds than the typical face-to-face venues. They can be recorded, too, though you must get written permission from anyone who speaks during the recording to post readings online.

For face-to-face readings, secure a venue well ahead of time. For either type, put together a calendar, one that includes the send date for social media posts and email announcements as described in Chapter 2. Invite your readers well ahead, a month at least, via email. Write all the details down so they know what is being asked for and so they don't forget—including the amount of time you are giving them to read: ten minutes? Fifteen? Decide and be clear. Put the readers' names on postings/posters and get them to send you a recent bio. *Send reminders to your readers and the staff the day before*—and include any last-minute changes. (And they better not be big changes, as your people have had to make their lives fit the plan.) Again, remind your readers of the time you have scheduled for them to read their work and let them know who else has been invited to read, too.

Readers invited to share their work should be honored that you have thought of them. Most do. New readers (new writers) might not realize that other people are reading too—that the event isn't all about them, though their level of nervousness about their own performance might be hard to cut through. When readers—new or practiced—arrive to an event, do their bit, and simply leave, well, this is rather rude. Remember this: introduce your readers to other people when they arrive. Readers should stay and hear other readers present their work. They are more likely to stay if they feel welcomed. Just like people have given them their attention, they should show that they are part of the total event and can offer their attention too. If you are inviting a new writer, let them know the scope of the event and politely suggest that they practice reading in the allotted time, perhaps, and that they bring family or friends to the reading. (Always suggest to the readers that they bring people if they can—and make those people welcome too.) Let the readers know that the event has a schedule and that you will be pleased to introduce them to the other people involved. Then be sure to do that.

Be sure to prepare your MC with all the info they need to keep the event moving at start, finish, and between readers: is the submission period open? What kind of merchandise is for sale at the table in the back (or front)? (See "Book Fairs and Table Events" below, on putting together a table.) Did the readers all send in a reasonable bio and does the MC have those and can they clearly read the text on stage? Is there adequate light at the mic? Is the mic adequate? Are everyone's phones charged if they are reading that way? What's being raffled? Who is selling tickets? (It better be someone who can play the crowd.) Make a plan (ahead!) with the MC and staff so all these mentions are coordinated with the table and the staff in the audience. If you are selling books by the author, be ready with those (and a sign with the price) and the cash to make change or the card reader connected to your bank account. Make sure the MC is someone lively. Everyone gets nervous up there, so who can be charming and funny while stressed? You will find out.

Make sure everyone gets thanked, too. At the mic, in person, hopefully both. If possible, remind the crowd about the next reading: date, time, and place.

For online readings it is similar. We all know the drill on etiquette with Zoom readings. Some people like the video function off during a reading, others like audience videos on—at least discuss ahead with staff. During the reading, everyone should turn their mics off except the reader—the MC should ask for that. The MC, as above, should be prepared with organizational info (including a link to buy books, perhaps) and bios, ready with everything they need to ferry everyone through the experience. The online MC has to listen closely, as well, for any cues to change, such as reacting quickly enough if a reader's connection fails. (Talk to the audience about organizational info, perhaps, while the person reconnects.) Have a backup person, beyond the MC, to deal with tech issues—give their email/phone numbers to the readers, for problem-solving texts during the event. This is vital, having someone who can monitor the technical functions during a reading. This should be someone who can also check the organization email during the event in case there is a problem that someone is trying to get the organizers to understand. That tech person (or persons) can also monitor the chat function, manage the recording, and even communicate with the MC via text to point them in one direction or the other, privately, should it become obvious that certain attention is needed.

A quick mention on speaking and pronouns. Make sure your MC and anyone else who will be speaking during an event (online or in person) have been informed on the preferred pronouns of your participants. Ask everyone ahead. On your emails, for instance, while you are communicating to set up an event, put your pronouns underneath your name on the closing. Make it obvious that you are noticing such things are important and that you would like to respect the speakers' wishes. You really should do the same with any correspondence.

A quick note on inside jokes during a reading: avoid them. If your MC is inclined to call someone/something out or make a sly reference to specific individuals or situations that no one else will "get"—just don't. For one, you are leaving the audience to wonder, which makes the audience feel like they are not really being included in the event. At minimum it distracts everyone from the moment at hand, inviting most of the audience to take their attention elsewhere. At worst, people won't return since the event seems to be for limited interest. To be sure you don't misunderstand: *always* include a thank you at the end of your readings to acknowledge all the people who put work into the event but might not be visible on the screen or stage.

And finally, on keeping the focus: the same problem of inside jokes applies to interviews that happen after a writer reads from their work, where the audience might be invited to ask questions though primarily the point is to listen to the writer in conversation with the MC. In too many of these cases, we end up watching the interviewer and writer replay their close personal connection—self congratulate, giggle, whatever. This is simply not as interesting as hearing the writer answer questions that are of interest to the audience—about the writing, the inspiration and connection to their other writing, or the thoughts about the subject matter they chose, etc. Don't make an audience sit through your private compliments and memories—it can be embarrassing to watch. Instead, save those for later and make sure the interview questions are well thought out and prepared ahead.

Launch Party

Most literary magazines that publish annually, semiannually, or even quarterly, celebrate each new issue with a launch party. Contributors can be invited to read and staff might do the introducing with stories from the trenches. "We chose the poem by our next reader during a meeting that took place after some recent fires so we began looking for submissions that address climate change." It's fun to meet the writers whose work you've admired, and they get a chance to thank you for your attention.

If it's a face-to-face event, up the party angle! Depending on the focus of that issue, a reading in an unusual location (maybe a park, but perhaps an auto-shop or a VFW Hall) can bring in new listeners or refocus the "usual crowd" on a wider community of writers. You can also have your online MC in an unusual location—keep the audience engaged by changing things up. If you are face-to-face, bring snacks, or buy them from the venue if you are at a place that serves food and drinks—discuss a budget and place your order ahead of time with the manager. You can get a good deal from a restaurant with a nice patio or event room by bringing in people who will also order other items from the regular menu. Make sure you get a venue with a large open area, plenty of seating, with good ventilation and good sound. Do not bring food to a restaurant or bar that already serves food—this is beyond rude. Want a celebratory cake? Ask if the restaurant/bar makes cakes and if they don't be sure you discuss ahead with the venue's contact person about bringing a cake and serving it. Try props and balloons. Whatever makes it special. Take photos (well, always take photos) and get ahead of the event with social media.

By all means, invite the writers from the issue to read. (See above, on scheduling readers and preparing them.) Create a banner from the artwork of the present issue and put it on email announcements and social media platforms. Get buy-in—plan a raffle, too, raise some money. Tell staff and contributors to stop by and get their complimentary copies. You can even give an artist from the issue a moment to talk about their work (make sure they practice—new artists, especially, need to prepare their remarks just like writers do). Invite your donors and the board. Avoid open mics during launch parties—unless you want to have your editors read a tiny bit and give the audience an idea of what kind of writers are doing the editing. Have the new issue of the magazine front and center at the merch table or available for sale from your website at the click of a link. Never hold a launch party if the issue is not there—get your printing schedule in order. Remember to invite the chair of your department, your favorite faculty, and maybe even the dean who either does contribute funding or might want to.

For online launch parties, the above is similar though you might have to be more creative on the details of celebrating that particular issue. You can have editors read snippets of their favorite pieces, for instance. You might invite readers to send a video file of themselves reading from the selection you published at an interesting spot or in an interesting way. These videos have to be edited and curated for real function—this is where you need an audio/video editor. You can run a raffle that is essentially a quiz at the end for the audience. Who paid really good attention and can answer these five funny questions? You win a book! Get creative.

An undergrad literary magazine is a community in itself and nurturing that community of friends and colleagues can often be one of the best ways for that lit mag to better nurture the larger literary community. Hosting events, contests, open mics, social events—an undergrad literary magazine can be so much more than the invaluable and wonderful publication the team creates at the end of it all. We have the opportunity to reflect on the amazing aspects of our literary community way beyond the actual publication.

—John Lyons, Drama Editor (2020–2021), *earthwords: the undergraduate literary review*, University of Iowa

Open Mic

These are so simple and fun—but you must have a firm and funny MC, to start. Firm for timing (three-minute max, for instance, or whatever you decide) and funny for avoiding the inevitable awkward moments. Make a clear sign-up list with the rules written out and a limited number of spaces available. Only what you can handle—and what the audience will stand for. For online, put this in the chat. For face-to-face make sure the mic and the venue are working and set up properly and that everyone can hear and be heard—test everything ahead. Have the MC *explain the rules at the mic before you start*. Should I say that again? Yes, repeat the rules. REPEATEDLY. Have a designated person *with a timing device* help the MC keep time. Use your phone. Let the readers know they will hear this sound (beep) or see this light over here (shine), when their time is up and they must finish within thirty seconds. Make sure your MC never shames anyone but can deal with humor and effective insistence about everyone respecting the space and time. That said, open mics, even online, are best when they are a little more informal and personal. Someone trips over pronunciation or their phone swallows the text for a moment? The audience can offer some encouragement. Assure the new reader that you can withstand a glitch for the pleasure of hearing their first reading experience. Thank each person. Another round of applause. Give a special round of applause to everyone who is reading before a live audience for the first time.

If you would like some music at your events and know some musicians, invite them to contribute during an open mic too. You might have to arrange a bit of this ahead of time—contact the musician(s) and let them know what you are looking for and see if they are willing to join. Perhaps test the online platform for the event during a practice session to check the computer mics and sound quality. If you start inviting musicians and it works out, after a while word will get out and you might not have to arrange ahead.

Slam

Put on some comfortable clothes for this one because there will be some moving around at your average slam. You've probably never in all your life yelled so loud at a competition that wasn't commercial sports. Slams are soooo fun. They are invigorating and really special word fests—your poets and writers are belting out their best and the audience better let them know it. Slams bear no relation to the typical quiet order of a classroom or formal reading—thank goodness. Again, a slam MC is a very special person, ready to rev the crowd and give the performers their due space. Ask a faculty person or local writer to MC or judge. You need at least three judges if you are doing a traditional slam, with scoring. Make sure you have reasonable judges (and people who won't mind getting yelled at) with all the necessary rules spelled out ahead. Make sure the crowd has some ground rules too, spelled out by the MC, on disagreements or huge love. No one is allowed on stage except the readers and the MC. Do not touch the judges! Have a reliable score-keeper and lots of water. Hold on tight, keep the rounds going, and get ready to spread some respect.

And you can do it online, though mics can get overwhelmed with the decibels, and the people in your house who are not online might need to be warned about what's going on.

Performance

Performances in general—in person, at an appropriate venue—can be very creative. Is there an amphitheater on campus? An interesting wide hallway on the tenth floor where thirty people can sit or stretch out on the carpet? Does your theater department have a script-writing award and can your staff stage a reading? Are there composers and musicians at your university? Having musicians and writers collaborate on a performance can be incredible. Onsite visual arts with wordplay alongside, time-based art confabulations in person or online? Give it a try.

If your magazine publishes music or theater online (or produces CDs or streams video or audio on a website or YouTube channel) you may need some production help. The videos or recordings, after all, are only as good as the production value. It doesn't matter, really, how good it was in person if that goodness is blurred or buzzy. Students frequently want to include recordings in their publication efforts, but the work to do so is considerable. Make your way quickly to the nearest Communications Department and find some student producers. Or find the faculty member who teaches production and ask them. Give another student a chance to practice what they are learning. And if hosting recorded content is going to be a regular thing, give that student producer a title—Director of Performances, perhaps, or Audio Content Producer. Something accurate that can also go on a resumé. And remember that if you aren't willing to sit through the entire recording, no one else will be either.

Equipment can be a major factor with producing or recording performances. Many colleges and universities have places (Student Events, Library, etc.) where you can check out video or recording equipment (ask around), but you often have to be part of a department, registered in a certain class, etc. You might be able to hire someone who already has equipment. Here's the biggest problem with using your own budget to buy equipment (other than finding someone who can actually use it well): it walks away. Unless you have a staff person who is completely responsible and dependable, do not, ever, just send someone off with the video camera or recording equipment. No one wants to feel really angry at that irresponsible person who misplaced the expensive stuff. No one wants to have to buy that video camera again. And again. Or never again. Make sure your phone doesn't go on overnights. Also, check to see if there is cloud storage space at your institution to house the files while they are being edited. These files are likely too large to pass around via email.

When you host performances or include them (or produce recordings) be sure that everyone involved is on the same page about what is being done and why. Make sure the venue works. Be clear on all the parameters: scheduling the slot, checking for needed lighting, reminding everyone, explaining the expectations. Do a rehearsal, if you possibly can. If you include musicians at a reading, be sure the music is appropriate. An entire rock-and-roll band cannot set up between a poet and fiction writer reading a few pages of their work, not to mention that the sound levels can blow your audience away. Instead, consider a rap artist whose a cappella vocal tones might be friendly to your audience's ears. Some of these extra steps might scare you away from including performances, but don't be put off—it's something different and good performances can make your event, website, or publication really memorable.

Book Fairs and Table Events

I'm using "book fair" as a general term, meaning any event where you might have a table—including at your readings or other events. At book fairs you are there along with many other publishers, community literary organizations, artists' collectives, etc. You get to know these other organizations, and they get to know you. Book fairs can be attached to festivals, conferences, annual meetings, or activity fairs at your college or university. Your table would probably feature your latest issue and some copies of previous volumes, maybe include a laptop that passersby could scroll through to get a mental picture of your website, T-shirts, or book bags—whatever you sell or give away. Free bookmarks or pencils or pens with the organization's email address or web address are helpful to remind people that they need to look you up when they get home.

Promotional material—swag. Very helpful. Often inexpensive. Bookmarks are very effective and easy to transport. Use your logo and have fun with the design and text. Include a catchy phrase and the relevant icons of your social media sites. People who pick up bookmarks, and who you talk to, are likely to look you up online. Include important dates (submission deadlines or readings) and/or general information (your journal's subtitle or email/ physical university address). Keep it tasteful. I have seen instances where poorly designed or badly thought out wording or images on swag incited the *wrong* sort of attention. Remember that you may have to work with university branding. Ask your faculty advisor if university approval will be required for whatever swag you produce.

For staffing a table, try to schedule reasonable blocks of time. Make sure the staff members know how to keep records for sales. Be sure the cash box has a reasonable amount of change—and that the staff has downloaded on their phones the correct card swipe reader info (your organization's bank account, not just anyone's personal bank info). Have a decent tablecloth, and a banner that can be attached to the front of a standard table. (Get a banner printed, a reusable tarp banner with a plastic coating made for your magazine's events—one that can be taped, washed off, and reused; put only the journal's name and logo on the banner, so it is reasonable for a wide variety of events over time.) Put together, a week ahead, a spreadsheet with everyone's time slot and contact info in case there are changes at the last moment. Send this to all concerned, and update everyone. Remind them the day before.

For tabling, always include a sign-up sheet (data collection—names and emails) so people who stop by and talk can be contacted about other events. And be sure to input those new addresses in your mail-handling program when you get back to the office. Print out a list of prices, maybe prepare handouts advertising events and/or submissions guidelines, bring a few book easels to show off your latest issues, and include whatever table bling would fit the theme of the event. Don't forget the scissors, extra paper, tape, pens, etc.

This all sounds like a lot, but here's a good trick: get yourself a rolling bag, like teachers use, or a simple carry-on bag that people use for airplane travel, and put all these tabling items inside. Keep it somewhere safe if the cash box is inside or put the cash box somewhere else safe and add it just before you leave for the event. Have some clipboards and extra sharpies in there, a couple of rolls of tape and some blanks of your open mic sign-up sheet, some staff applications—basically anything you might need. Once you get this bag all set up, it will save you time. Just pick it up and go, restock it when you get back to the office, make your bank deposit from cash sales if you have any, and make sure the bag is all set for next time. Voilà!

Last thing: anyone sitting at the table should have at least some knowledge of the magazine and should be friendly enough to talk to just about anyone who comes by. "Hi, have you seen our journal? Issue number 32 just came out!" If someone looks like a teacher you might ask if his/her/ their students would be interested in submitting—pass along a bookmark or three. Make no assumptions, of course, and be ready, and certainly take cues from whoever shows up about how much they are willing to find out or whether they were just being polite and need to keep walking through.

Again, remember to make a staff schedule for tabling at least a week ahead. No one wants to sit for eight hours. Remind everyone the day ahead. Give everyone the schedule along with contact info for everyone else who is on the schedule. Have one person in charge who can at least monitor throughout the day.

Your school might sponsor an event for all student organizations at the start of a semester or academic year—this is a great place to find students who like creative writing no matter what their home department.

It's all about visibility. Also, if you are an official student organization, you probably have some web space available on the student activities, university, or college website. Make sure the info is up to date, complete, and attractive. This isn't exactly "tabling" but it could substitute for a physical gathering and mean the type of ready visibility and connection you need.

Busking

Have you ever done poetry or flash fiction busking? It's fun for those who write well under pressure. Bring some good copier paper and a couple of manual typewriters (make sure they are functional and have plenty of ribbon) to your next tabling event and schedule some creative types to write quick poems and stories on demand. Busking is usually quite popular with the crowd at farmers' markets and literary events. Make sure you have enough people to do this *and* handle inquiries about your magazine from the crowds walking by. People get a kick out of a "personal" poem or story. Ask them for a subject, their name so you can connect the person with the final product, and never their phone numbers—that's too personal. Ask the person for maybe a situation. Again, be cautious and sensitive—don't say/ write rude things or make assumptions; you should do a bit of training with the busking crew. Maybe even have your audience member fill out a quick form with genre, topic, key words, and name—and remind them to come back in ten minutes for the result. (No one wants to be stared at while they try to compose on the spot under great pressure to satisfy.) You can also ask for donations in exchange for these quick poems and stories—raise a little cash to get your swag produced. At least put out a tip jar.

Panels

If you are asked to join a panel at a literary event, you are being asked to represent your journal as a professional. There is typically a topic (having to do with journal production or editing, or etc.) and you prepare something to say. Make sure you know what is expected, what the topic is, maybe what others are going to talk about, and please don't bore the audience to death with slow, meaningless, or empty-effusive replays of your worst day on the job. When you are asked to speak about your literary journal or your job as an editor, be professional, direct, and informative. Remember those fiction writers who read way past their allotted time at the open mic? Time your presentation and keep strictly within the boundaries. Talk to the audience, not a page or phone—or at least stop to speak directly to the audience, and informally, a couple of times.

If you are hosting a panel (on some aspect of writing or editing or publishing), organize it with care and intent. Have a direct purpose (a focus) and make sure you communicate all the important details to the panelists.

You might ask your board, department faculty, or community connections to find appropriate people for your panel—writers or specialists who have something important to add. Remember to think of the scope and the diversity of opinions on the topics—don't have four people all saying the same thing, clutching tightly to the same lens. A diversity of experiences and ideas will probably make the discussion lively and memorable.

When you discuss a special event, like a lunchtime panel, at your weekly organizational meeting, remind everyone that the discussion is (a) preliminary (start by discussing whether you want to do it) moving on to (b) planning (how are you going to do it and what is everyone's job?) and (c) final stages (is everything in place?). Make sure everyone knows that they can't just go out and ask their friends to join the panel when the exact participants haven't been decided on yet. This happens a lot. We had one student who suggested her aunt for just about every event on the docket— not that her aunt wasn't a lovely person with plenty of literary credibility, but there were plenty of people in the community and beyond who were usually more appropriate. Balancing friends (people you know) and insiders with people less connected to your organization is a good idea, too—make new connections happen at your events, especially an event as personal and intense as a good panel discussion.

Are there issues facing the writers at your academic institution that might make for a good discussion? See if your department will cohost a panel on applying for graduate school, writing memoir versus fiction, or on neurodiversity and the writing life. Keep it real, get a room reservation through the department, advertise the event, and pass around a sign-in sheet at the event so you can add to your email lists. Serve lunch if you can— simple sandwiches. Or do it online and offer a slate of web links on the topic in the chat function.

Classes

You may be invited to talk to a class about what you do—about editing the journal or planning literary events, or even submitting new work and finding new staff. How does your job as an editor intersect with the subject of the course? How long do you have to speak? Ask questions ahead and prepare your remarks. If you would like to visit a creative writing class at the start of the semester in order to elicit submissions or let people know about open staff positions, what can you tell the instructor about what you intend to say and how much time you need? Again, be direct, take the journal with you to pass around, or put links to the journal website in the chat function. End by asking if anyone has any questions. Pass out bookmarks or a small flier (copies done cheaply or an electronic file you can share) with pertinent info. If possible, get the instructor to send the web address of your journal to the students before your visit, so they can see what you are all about before you arrive—or write it on the board (or share on screen) while you are there. You might also put links to your submission guidelines and the website in the chat box if you are meeting online. Consider asking the faculty member, at a later time, about writers in the class that the faculty member would recommend for a reading event.

Conferences

This is a big subject—too big to fully describe here. Student literary journals who have staff attend conferences or put on their own conferences have to have resources and a solid organizational structure with plenty of institutional support. While sending everyone to a conference is a lot easier and probably a lot more fun, putting on a small conference is incredibly rewarding and will provide you a lifetime of lessons on literary endeavors, programming, and workplace culture—and the kind of team you are capable of building.

A conference should have a focus. AWP maintains a list of Writers' Conferences & Centers (https://www.awpwriter.org/wcc/overview) along with a searchable function to narrow results. You can use this list to get an idea of the variety of opportunities for writers already available in your area.

The Boldface Conference for Emerging Writers at University of Houston is run by undergraduate editors (and their graduate advisor and faculty advisor) and takes place in May, about two to three weeks after the end of Spring semester. There are featured writers who give a variety of talks and readings and join panels for the final day—panels devoted to issues of professionalism in literary publishing. The first four days are devoted to workshops. Graduate students from the creative writing program run small group workshops and also present craft talks. Undergraduates come from all over the United States to attend, and community writers from the metropolitan area attend too. The focus of Boldface is *new writers* and the writing process—how to support and maintain your writing. The featured writers are usually recently published and have a book or two. They've been working hard and can talk about their process, how they got started. The conference is held at the M.D. Anderson library, the university's library, so the space is free of charge but the journal's staff has to set up and clean up (unpack and pack everything out every day). It's a lot of work, but the registration fees pay the student editors for their work, editors who otherwise get no stipend or tuition forgiveness the rest of the year.

When the pandemic hit, the conference went online. The students called the online version the ~~Strikethrough~~ Workshop. The focus was writers "striking through" the pandemic's upheaval—a one-time solution. More featured writers were invited because they didn't have to travel or stay in hotels. The money stretched a bit. After going through a very quick planning stage at the end of March/early April, the undergraduate editors launched the new conference with announcements on their website and social media platforms, plus a press release. They moved it back one week and ended up having more participants than the face-to-face conference. Participants signed up from as far away as Nigeria, Mexico, France, and Canada. This year (2021) the student editors are returning to the Boldface Conference but online, making further changes that speak to the moment we are currently in where more people are used to online gatherings.

The online format for events and meetings is of course being tested everywhere now—for all of us, by all of us. A lot has to be worked out for the literary community in the long run, and many of us are tired of screens. But there are so many new discoveries, too. Online readings can reach many more people. Small group discussions are relatively reasonable on a laptop screen. The experience of shifting the writing conference to an online format certainly showed the students at Houston that possibilities exist out there, in this changed world, and that challenges can be met by creative thinkers with new technologies.

Other Creating Writing Opportunities

As an editor and leader of an organization whose purpose is to promote literary works, you have an opportunity (and some credibility) to promote other events that help the community at large experience the work that you and your editors, readers, and writers do—like writing. Though you may be invited to bring your magazine to a book fair or literary event in your area or state where you can advertise your submission period or sell copies, you may also decide to buy space at events like that where table space is something you purchase. You can have your staff do some poetry busking at a Saturday market or you can send a writer (or staff member) to read at an event that includes other readers who are editors from other literary concerns. Invites to join other editors are common and a good way to showcase the excellent creative work of your editing staff. You can run some workshops on a Sunday afternoon ("How to Submit Your Work to Literary Magazines Online") or publish craft texts for writers. Video lectures on craft can be posted on your website. (Be certain to get permission if you do this—written permission from the speaker.) You may also get to nominate student writers for prizes or internships. You are a literary magazine, so nominate your readers for national award like the Pushcart Prizes (http://pushcartprize.com/nomination.html). In other words, as a literary magazine you can promote writers and writing in a number of ways other than by single publications of poems and stories and essays and art.

Every state, every region, has writers and literary journals. If an editor of a literary journal at another college or university—or a community literary magazine—is within a couple of hours drive, you might consider inviting that editor to your university to give a talk on writing and editing. Perhaps ask them to talk about a subject of the moment like "How to Assess Fairness and Diversity at Your Magazine." (Make sure they have something helpful to say on the subject first, of course.) By informing your organization, your staff, the students at your institution, you are creating new opportunities for their writing by helping them find out where their voices might be appreciated and how they might go about shaping or formatting their work to the markets that are available to them—locally or beyond.

So much of what we call "writing" has to do with the ethics and practices of the literary world. And by this I mean everything from the standard use of dialogue tags to manuscript formatting and submission fees. We can easily see the decades and decades of standardized practices (margin sizes, header and footer requirements, institutional style books, etc. etc.)—plus those that have come under scrutiny and been changed (last week, last year, or five years ago). Literary realism and narrative poetry are not the only games in town anymore. When a new writer is apprised of all this detail, all these possibilities, they get to choose whether to engage in those avenues or methods or whether they want to branch out—and they also get to hear about the opportunities that result from those choices, often through social media. However it plays out, a writer can move their writing forward once they know something about what's on the path ahead. (Too often in creative writing programs there is a competitive vibe rather than a commitment to assist, to moving everyone forward. This does not help most writers orient themselves to their work, to building a relationship between themselves and the page.) As a student journal that is interested in new writers, you may be able to help with the transition to a more public venue for the literary citizens in your hemisphere by being a nexus of conversation on current topics. And don't just talk. Editors are more conscious of having a positive impact on the diversity of work being chosen for publication. But what about also having more diverse editors doing the choosing? Creating opportunities for everyone will also mean listening to writers, editors, and slush-pile readers discuss the ethics and parameters of their interests.

Editors can also use the structure of the literary magazine to help the staff move their creative work forward by starting writing groups among the ranks, or sending out weekly or monthly writing prompts to the whole staff—and then holding smaller events where the results can be shared. Efforts like this tend to fall off as semesters progress and workloads increase, but good first drafts can get generated with relatively little effort in making the space for it. If your editing staff has a Slack account, for instance, their creative work could be linked on a thread devoted to prompts and drafts; their posted work can be visited or revisited, discussed and revised, as time allows.

Awards can help you raise money—if they are run with enough PR to garner the attention they need in order to serve the organization. Chapter 4 has more information on awards. Awards are writing opportunities, sure, but

The Write-a-Thon at the University of Houston began as a fundraiser for the summer Boldface Conference, run by the undergraduate literary magazine. ("Be Bold—Face the Writer in You" was the motto.) The money raised was used to pay workshop leaders (graduate students in creative writing) and Featured Writers. The idea for Write-a-Thon was that each participant would get friends and family and neighbors and bosses to pay so much per hour for the writer to write. The organizers (the magazine's staff, basically) found people (community writers and creative writing faculty) to come and judge sonnet contests and flash fiction races. For years the conference managed to keep the cost of the conference under $100 for students by raising money in the fall. But it took a LOT of organizing to get writers to come to Write-a-Thon with a full list of people who were going to give them money to write. Not impossible, but you must have people who fully believe in the project. There were prizes for the writing contests—so the magazine's staff went out and got donations like gift certificates to grocery stores and bookstores. Over the years, the conference earned more institutional support and Write-a-Thon developed into a day for student and community writers to gather and write and show off their skills several months before the week-long conference.

what might be more correct about awards-as-writing-opportunities is that they help writers further revise, edit, or reimagine their work because they provide deadlines. Awards function for most writers as more motivational than as actual forward moment of a "career." For the winners, they can be both. While certain awards do launch new writers, those writers survive and thrive because they keep writing (most of them) without constant approbation.

University Engagement: Admissions, Alumni Relations, and Development

Depending on your profile at your university or college, you may be a winning asset for other university offices like Admissions or Alumni Relations—even the fundraisers might crack a smile when they see you coming. After all, you are the very definition of engaged learning. The fact that you can manage a production process and create a visible product—your magazine and also your events—means that you can manage the workplace. The arts angle doesn't hurt either—you are arbiters of the moment. And writing—who doesn't love a person that artfully manages communication? The professionalization of your journal, of your course of study in literature perhaps, is a valuable asset to those at the university who want to show prospective students (or alum with deep pockets) that your institution creates fantastically talented graduates.

Don't underestimate your value—and don't take it for granted either. You do the work, you claim the credit. If you give the Admissions Office a box of your latest issue (to distribute to prospective students interested in studying writing or literature), ask the Admissions staff to show up at an event. Offer to show visiting prospective students the journal's office or have them come to a meeting or to one of your readings. On the alumni side, perhaps you can help with an event or offer to find a poem by a student to be included in their alumni newsletter. You can create an event at homecoming or invite alums from your department to an online launch party. If you visit the Development Office to talk about finding a donor, bring materials (previous issues) and a clear, written description of what money you are looking for and why.

You are potentially quite valuable to your institution, but you are also responsible for creating and maintaining that value. Becoming a literary citizen, working as an editor for a student literary magazine and doing the job well, is not easy. It is incredibly valuable work for students who want to get some professional experience with literary organizations and/or nonprofit outfits. While I can keep listing a number of things for you to do, the reality is that I have listed too many things for one organization. You will have to pick and choose and make your own map—and no doubt you will come up with better things that appropriately fit you and your organization. Always remember that parts of citizenry are easy—making connections and creating opportunities is usually pretty simple. Follow-up is harder. Maintenance is sometimes easy, sometimes a pain. Everyone has their strong points and their weaknesses. Just keep it real and don't overextend yourselves.

6

Networking and Professionalization

Clearly one of the best things about working in a leadership position for an undergraduate literary magazine is that you get work experience—plus a taste of what it's like to program professional activities. This kind of leadership experience is not commonly available for undergraduates seeking Bachelor degrees, or not within the structure of the usual curriculum. Student literary magazine activities are usually extracurricular but invaluable for the institution and for students looking forward to the workplace. Most especially, you get to practice creating the kind of workspace you would find comfortable and productive.

Perhaps that is why so many undergraduates who are lifelong readers lean toward editing, even when there is no stipend. Of course you can't underestimate the fun of creating a working group and getting things done—in some cases, things that no one ever thought they could actually do. I have heard countless students muse on the enjoyment of connecting with people who are also engaged in an activity they value highly. So many students find out that they are really good at something. And who doesn't like getting credit? As a person in charge, you find your strengths and weaknesses. Or people point them out to you—don't forget to listen. You get to practice in a rather (not completely) low stakes environment. In the best situation, with reasonable institutional support and a system that's not hopelessly in defense mode (I'm thinking hurricanes and fires and pandemics), you get to build a work environment that brings everyone along and up. (Actually, I've seen students start publications in response to a hurricane—*Shards* https://shards.glassmountainmag.com/came from a desire to publish stories, poems, and artwork inspired by the aftermath of Hurricane Harvey.) Even in the toughest situations, networking and professionalization will provide an opportunity to start something new, to find uses for your creative energy. And while professionalism means developing your own working skills, networking is something you share in the process of developing your professional profile—please, please, remember to always share.

Networking (making connections) happens not only for you but for others around you. First your staff, then other people right outside your immediate sphere, perhaps students who are not editors or readers for your journal but are students in your department, let's say, who might submit work. These are people who are influenced by what you are doing. I'm counting here the organizations you work with in the community—the university or college community or the local/regional community groups. Otherwise, it's not really networking so much as knitting a straight line. Multiple connections in many directions will hold the organization up in rough times and make it fly in the best of times. Don't be selfish with your connections, but do honor them by working nicely with the people involved—even those who are having a bad day.

As you move forward professionally in the future—no matter exactly where or in what professional line—the connections you make while working with an undergraduate literary magazine can help you find a place for yourself among others. Internships can lead to jobs. Connections can help you understand what it feels like to build a career, what works and doesn't in a particular situation (or for you) and why. Remember that all of these activities I am calling networking and professionalization keep you and your organization alive, functioning, and healthy. They also help you enter the workforce.

Keep updated contact lists (email, phone, and website) at all times: staff, writers, former readers, former contributors, etc. Make sure the staff helps with updating and knows how to use these lists and when to use them. Mailchimp (follow the rules!) will work to organize contact lists for particular activities: submission calls, readings (local and virtual may be different lists), etc. You may need a spreadsheet for all the info you find—the phone numbers of people and offices you work with at your institutions or in the local community, their social media accounts, useful hashtags, websites for community calendar schedules. Have a clipboard ready at all events (pen in hand) and don't forget to input, after the event is over, the info you get from people you meet. Keep in touch with everyone who crosses your path (well, maybe not everyone...). And never harass people with too many emails or postings (postings are easier to ignore, of course.) Answer your emails in a timely manner and post about your events with other literary organizations—give them a nod and help amplify their events. A year ago Instagram stories were the hot new thing, now it's TikTok, and tomorrow it will be something else. Use it all and use it wisely. Remember to thank the people who help you stay connected.

State and Local Writing Groups and Literary Organizations

It can be daunting to look at the national literary situation, imagining your way into it and making your organization matter to the huge and complex industry that is hundreds of years of mass publishing of the written word. It's a changing landscape, always changing, and the most recent grumblings may signal a long overdue need to publish the work of people who have been ignored for long enough. (Get to know the names of mid-sized publishers—and keep an eye on their lists.) Then think of the vast territory that is the internet, which is merely light meeting our eyeballs or sound waves touching the small bones in our ears. You can quickly feel overwhelmed by the numbers and complexity of contemporary communication. How do you fit? If you can do a few things very well, that's all you need. People around you find a niche all the time, and they do it by working in tandem with others and keeping an eye on where the opportunities are.

When it comes to professionalization and networking, start small. Try local literary organizations in your state, your county, your city/town. Closer to your end of the writing/publishing situation there are writing groups: people who share their creative work with a small number of other writers who have the intention of improving their craft—for themselves, purely, or perhaps for publication. They may have an online presence—collectives of many smaller groups sometimes maintain informational websites and conduct collective activities. No doubt there are people there who self-publish. If there is a Writers in the Schools group in your area, who is working there and how do they shape their public interface? These organizations usually hire local writers to visit classrooms and teach creative writing in K-12 schools, public and private. They may also invite writers for events, or host readings for the kids. Are there literary organizations that run workshops or host visiting writers for readings or interviews? Libraries (your university or a public library) often hold a reading series or host regular book-group meetings. Is there a local high school that offers creative writing classes and might those high school students benefit from hearing what creative writing is like for students at your college or university? You might be able to invite the students to one of your readings, and you could probably find a high school student to read their own work as a guest or at an open mic. You might have local writers that are engaged in any number of professional organizations (even as editors) that could benefit your organization by cosponsoring an event.

Ask your faculty about state-wide literary organizations. Visit your local independent bookstore. They often hold readings for writers with new books doing a book tour—and a lot of local bibliophiles attend. As mentioned, a used bookstore might have a workable space for a reading—your audience of students can shop the bargains afterward. And if you can find a coffee house (not a bar where everyone needs to be over twenty-one—don't even

I've seen editors succeed and fail for a variety of reasons. The best leaders are self-aware, self-reflective, curious, and questioning. Who knows, you may run another organization someday, based on what you do now. Support others and they will support you.

bother) with an open space (inside or out) where you can fit a crowd who will buy food and drinks, ask about a regular open mic night. Perhaps cosponsor with other literary organizations so you can share the workload—and learn a few things from them, too.

Most of the literary organizations mentioned in this book are nonprofits (see Chapter 1), and, as such, have a mission to provide an important service to the community. (Independent bookstores work with such low profit margins that they might as well be non-profits.) In other words, literary organizations run on a shoestring. Private businesses have a bottom line and might offer you a partnership that will essentially be a trade—for bringing in people who buy merchandise, food, or services. Be very cautious of venues that want to charge for space—even your school, as they should have venues for use by students that are not tied to payment. Recall the gift economy mentioned in Chapter 2—you can often trade your value (bringing students, editing skills, and web connections) with local literary-minded organizations. Run a writing contest together. A library holding a book fair might donate books to your organization for raffles you hold at readings. Your staff can probably make someone else's fundraising even more lively— bring your table, work the event wearing your matching T-shirts with the journal's name proudly printed, do some busking. Visit local high schools and help students put together chapbooks. Read to seniors. Volunteer to teach creative writing at an after-school program. Join Habitat for Humanity during winter break.

When you reach out to any of these organizations, you may or may not get a friendly response—or you may not get any response at all. Don't take it personally. People get busy, have good intentions, they even mistype email addresses. Write succinct messages—and answers—and work toward something clear as quickly as possible. If an idea or plan seems to catch some interest, suggest a meeting to work out the details. You will quickly learn what details can be worked out in an email exchange and which require people talking to each other privately or in groups. And if the idea won't work for you, be clear that you are declining the invitation and thank the person for the offer. When you are figuring out which partnerships to undertake, you will always have to figure out who the stakeholders are (the people who have a direct interest) and why. What's in it for them? What's in it for you? The warning here is not to make you suspicious, but to encourage you to be realistic and efficient—and to keep in mind that you will be graduating, moving on to other career activities.

Don't be taken advantage of—by anyone with a seemingly shiny object. In a way, this is a terrible warning because it might seem antithetical to the premise of this chapter, which is to look to the future and "join." But you must consider that anyone's interest may not always be the best for your organization. Always remember to parse through the new ideas that people bring to you and don't ever say "Yes" until you've run the idea by your staff and a few people with some experience. So often people bring Great New Ideas to student editors who see possibilities. "We can publish his book, right? This guy says he has a list of people who want to buy it. We might even make some money." "If we combine their conference with our conference, our budget with their name…" Pause a moment. Remember you are a nonprofit and you have a mission. You are, after all, representing the whole institution. Make sure your organization is not risking its good name but getting a positive push from the transaction. Aim at something you need or want, not something you can easily do without. Great Ideas can translate into a lot of bother, some sweat, and perhaps tears of disappointment. Be realistic. Listen closely to whomever is pitching an idea to you and ask a lot of questions. If it sounds interesting but doesn't quite fit, make counter offers (only if you really mean it). And you can always be polite (even grateful) when saying no. "Thank you so much for this great suggestion, but it doesn't fit our schedule right now. Let us know how it turns out." "Consider us for next year, perhaps?"

AWP and FUSE

You probably know other students interested in the literary arts at other colleges and universities. They might be doing work similar to yours. Many undergraduate literary magazines are housed in academia at departments (usually English or Languages) with creative writing programs. AWP (Association of Writers and Writing Programs https://www.awpwriter.org/) and FUSE (Forum for Undergraduate Student Editors https://www.fuse-national.com/) are two national organizations that can help you immensely. The latter, FUSE, has an annual conference on student editing (in the fall) and also holds an organizational meeting at the annual AWP conference which usually includes at least a dozen undergraduate journals. Both these events take place at various locations around the country—it's worth checking their websites to see if they are happening near you in the coming years.

FUSE https://www.fuse-national.com/national-undergraduate-student-jour is all about student journals and editing and can be incredibly useful for trading ideas and connecting with people who you may encounter in

Writing reviews of other undergraduate magazines for publication on the FUSE National website is a great way for students to publish writing, build up clips if they are interested in further exploring review writing, and connect with other undergraduate magazines—and for editors to get exposure for their journals.
—Jason Ferris, FUSE National Reviews Editor, 2019–2020,
Susquehanna University, Pennsylvania

publishing in the future. Your journal can send in proposals and present material on your particular experiences. The AWP annual conference is an event that most student editors enjoy attending for the plethora of literary activities from readings to panels on a huge variety of literary topics to the amazing book fair with upwards of 500 small publishers. Check out the website and their complete schedules of past meetings. https://www.awpwriter.org/

Conferences like AWP's and the FUSE conference are also opportunities to bring your journal to the attention of other new writers (be sure to take a flier with your submission guidelines or pass out bookmarks with the web address). AWP has scores of MFA programs attending their annual conference as well, so if any of your editors/writers are interested in graduate school AWP gives them a chance to make connections during the conference with students currently attending the programs they might consider applying to.

The conference experience (as your graduate or faculty advisors will tell you) can be enlightening—and fun, if you send a group of students who already know each other because they've been working together and can share the travel experience in a reasonable fashion. Moving around an enormous convention center at an AWP conference and encountering writers whose books you've read is exciting. I've seen students approach writers

Attending a conference can be fun—especially if you look at the schedule ahead of time and see which sessions and readings might be most interesting. If you are taking your journal, make a schedule so you can be sure the table is always staffed while everyone gets a chance to attend a few sessions. If you are attending online, have links ready so you can add a link to your website or "store" in the chat box. For travel, have the staff go over the travel and housing arrangements and put together some house rules (if you hire an Airbnb, for example) before you go—make sure everyone is comfortable and that no one ends up paying for something too expensive.

off the cuff with requests for interviews for their literary journals, or even visits for a reading series, and get positive responses. As these events move online, there will still be opportunities to learn a lot about the literary arts in the United States and beyond at virtual conferences. AWP tries to include an aspect of the international, but it still remains largely a US-focused conference. As these conferences take on new calls for social change—changes that many writers have been calling for over the decades—there will be new opportunities for many more types of writers and publishing opportunities. This year, for instance, AWP's virtual conference instated a policy for panels that favored new presenters, new voices in discussion.

A low-energy, minimally funded student literary magazine can certainly skip the more expensive conferences. Time is short and your time is worth a lot. But there are still the local and state literary events. Online workshops have gained popularity during the recent pandemic (see below). With a little research, you can find opportunities for your undergraduate literary magazine staff. The websites of so many literary organizations list scores of opportunities useful to student editors (internships, editorial positions, contests, craft talks)—visit the list at the back of this book.

National and International Conferences

How about having your staff attend local or regional (or even international) literature conferences? Assuming that a number of your staff members are studying literature, these conferences can help staff develop some individual networking, writing, and editing skills in the research realm. While travel can be costly, many literature conferences have recently moved to digital platforms and it's likely a significant number will remain so. The cost for various online literature conferences seems to be holding at regular registration fees for the time being—which in many cases is a bargain for the experience. Some literature conferences, by the way—like regional MLA conferences (Modern Language Association https://www.mla.org/)—have creative writing groups or sections that hold meetings or present panels featuring regional writers and publishers.

Some creative writing programs offer students an opportunity to attend conferences by offering funding for travel or registration fees. When academic programs sponsor or support local or state writing or literature conferences there may be free student registrations available. Ask your department chair, advisor, or program director. Also, be sure to check with the office of student activities if your organization is a registered student organization and has access to money from student fees—they sometimes pay for or reimburse the organizations for travel/registration expenses.

AWP, mentioned above, has a searchable database of literary centers from all over the world that offer a variety of services to writers and editors (Writers' Conferences and Centers [WC&C] is the umbrella organization and the searchable database is the Directory of Conferences and Centers https://www.awpwriter.org/wcc/directory_conferences_centers) This list—which can be filtered by state, region, or country—is a listing of only the writing conferences and centers that are paid members of this AWP list. So the entries are not exhaustive but many of the tried and true conference (plus some interesting newcomers) are listed there—as well as major writing centers from all over the U.S. If your journal puts on a conference, AWP's WC&C offers a number of services to help you get the word out—plus you get a page on the site to highlight your basic info (keep it updated!). You might consider joining the WC&C Directory if you are planning to offer a conference or workshop weekend year after year.

Concerning writing centers, many of these offer short-term (a day or weekend) or longer-term (ten- or twelve-week) writing or editing workshops. You will probably have a few of these literary hubs in your town, city, or state (see above). Some may focus on poetry, others on commercial fiction writing, sci-fi or fantasy, or young adult fiction. While fees for community workshops have traditionally been out of the realm for students, many of these workshops have moved online and some have reduced the fees since the overhead is lower. Your journal could offer something like a community workshop—with the appropriate planning and support.

A final note on international summer workshops. These have gained real traction in the past couple of decades, mostly due to the international travel aspect of the experience (colleges and universities love that). Travel is on hold for the moment, of course, but we might assume that such conferences

Boldface, the summer conference at University of Houston (https://www.boldfaceconference.com/), has been running for twelve years and hosts writers (both community and undergraduate) from all over the country for reduced cost. This conference focuses on the craft of writing with the final day spent on professional issues—panels and meetings on publishing, navigating the writing life, editing, and current issues in the literary world. What makes this conference possible is a number of resources: a graduate program in creative writing (graduate students teach as well as regular faculty), a big city with a literary arts scene, the ability and will to do some fundraising—plus an administration friendly to the arts and a board of advisors who help out. As mentioned earlier, the conference moved online for what we thought would be a single year. The one-time ~~strikethrough~~ Workshop (https://glassmountainmag.com/strikethrough/) was hugely successful, though that kind of event will no doubt evolve in the coming years. Keep your eyes open—there may be plenty of opportunity for you to innovate in the realm of conferences for new writers.

will rise again. Combining the two—international travel plus a focus on the craft of writing—has been one of the most popular conference experiences I've heard students talk about. The online environment makes it even easier for students from across the globe to connect, which is a silver lining to the pandemic situation. I hope many of you will get the chance, either way: traveling to connect, or staying home to do the same.

Internships

Some colleges and universities require their undergraduates to take an internship for credit (or no credit) as a requirement for the major. Others simply have internships available as a kind of work experience. Ask your advisor or inquire at the department office. For whatever reason, internships can be simple (you make coffee and answer phones all day) or incredibly rewarding (you get a full view of what it's like to do the thing you always thought you wanted to do). In some cases, the organization or business loves you so much that they offer you a job when you graduate—not always, but it happens.

Under certain conditions your magazine might also be able to offer internships. This is a good way to get extra help. (You might even be able to get a work-study student, though this is even rarer and probably depends on the department getting the work-study student and then committing some of their time to your journal's office.) There is usually a faculty member assigned to handle internships. You might want to initiate a discussion.

More and more creative writing programs are connecting students to summer internships—and some literary concerns, including publishers, offer these internships for summer or even full terms during the school year. Check the websites of mid-sized literary publishers and university publishers who have literary imprints. Interested in running your own nonprofit literary organization some day? (See Conferences and Centers, above.) Perhaps there is an internship available at a writer's retreat and you could apply. Check with your advisor or department office to see if you might be able to earn credit for an internship that you arrange yourself.

Here's the thing with internships: they are a type of training for self-starters. Ask your department or program for the guidelines that would satisfy their requirements and make sure the internship you create really counts. Looking for an internship is a type of training for a job hunt, frankly. And don't be discouraged if you find a place where you'd like to intern and it doesn't work out. A lot of organizations don't like to offer internships because setting it all up and getting someone up to speed can take so much time and bother that it's not worth it. If you find yourself out looking for an internship (some departments require that you interview for the internship, whether you find the internship yourself or not) be sure to be extremely professional: dress well, listen up, be succinct and direct, and show up on time.

In some cases you might find paid internships—or your program might have an endowment that funds an internship. This is helpful, of course, but even paid internships rarely provide anything close to a living wage. In other words, choose your internship wisely because you are actually spending your resources to do this "job." Experience is the point, and even the intern that makes coffee and delivers mail gets a glimpse of what it's like to be part of a business or organization. (The workers who do the less-prized work often see the reality of a business concern better than anyone.) Plus, you can find connections almost anywhere if you are a people person. So much of the work being described in this chapter is a function of being outgoing, observant, organized, and dependable. Internships are no exception.

Beyond the Undergrad Magazine Experience

Freelancing, Editing, Tutoring, and Finding Your Individual Way

So many former undergrad editors I know have gone on to do interesting things in the literary world, including start their own publishing companies. Aries Jones, the publishing coordinator at Night Heron Media, began her post-bac work in publishing when she saw her former internship coordinator from Bright Sky Press at a community reading. "How would like to come back to Bright Sky in a paid position?" the woman inquired. This started Aries on a path that has resulted in her starting her own publishing company along with another former colleague from Bright Sky. "Here at Night Heron, we are very aware that Houston's literary scene is really big. We are trying to find our niche, and sure it's a risk, but this is my dream job," she told me recently. Since she and her cofounder, Mike Vance, were most familiar with nonprofit work, Night Heron Media is a nonprofit. "We want to serve the literary community by offering services we saw no one else offering." This includes web and editing services. In another arm of the business, they publish children's books, but also books about Texas history and other Texas subjects. Aries is not looking toward big publishing, but local publishing and media models. "We want to be accessible to anyone finding their way in publishing," she said, going on to reminisce about her time as the Editor-in-Chief of *Glass Mountain Magazine* in 2015–2016. "I had never done anything like that before, despite the fact I was an avid reader growing up. First I was a fiction reader for the magazine. Then suddenly I was Editor-in-Chief—and I liked being in charge of the magazine. And editing? It turned out I loved it."

The managing editor during the same academic year, Mai Tram Nguyen, now runs her own business as well—Hestia Baking Company. "So much of what I learned running a student literary magazine is useful in running the bakery." She was referring to organization, maintaining contacts, running a website and social media accounts, financial planning, keeping a schedule, and bottom line energy. Mai had been a grade school teacher after her undergraduate work and had returned to university with an interest in linguistics. "I was going to go to graduate school but ended up joining *Glass Mountain* as a post-bac. Sure, I did a bit of everything—including layout of the magazine when we lost our graphics person a couple of weeks before production began. It all worked out. We had a really good team." I asked her if she would like to return to publishing. "Absolutely," she said. "I can see myself as an editor promoting the work of writers of color, women, and people who we aren't hearing from as much as we could. I like the idea of the integrity of the book and the writer over monetization." Mai let me know that she was still in touch with many editors from her year at the magazine—others were in graduate school, teaching English as a second language, or working as editors.

Aries Jones, in fact, has also worked as a freelance editor and tutor after graduating and mentioned the website Upwork (https://www.upwork.com/) as a place to find editing jobs. Over the years, I've seen a number of former student editors find work in freelance editing—and they make good money. There are in-house full-time editing jobs at large corporations, city, state, and federal offices. Think of all that web content out there. Someone has to edit all that text. And I can't think of a month passing when I haven't gotten a request via my Inbox from someone who needs an editor to work with on their memoir or family history—even on novels and biographies. Every writer out there needs an editor.

Tutoring pays well too—and during Covid there were a number of opportunities for college students and former college students to help families at home with the kids who were not going to school, people who needed help with all the online content. There are a number of websites that can connect you with opportunities for online tutoring for K-12 students. I've heard many current and former undergrad editors say that they like the personal nature of this one-on-one work. And much like freelance editing, you can pick up work when you want it or need it.

Freelance writing is another way to get some work and move toward your goal of living off your writing or editing. The climb is a little steeper these days for freelance writers—but if you have experience writing reviews, for instance, you have some material to show a prospective publisher along with the pitch for your story idea. Look at Indeed.com for a number of freelance (and full-time) writing and editing jobs that might work for you.

A life in literary publishing is not for everyone, of course, but establishing a career in academic publishing is what Allen Gee did after earning several degrees in writing and literature. (He is the author of *My Chinese-America*, an account of growing up in New York City's Chinatown and learning about all the stereotyping lenses that were being pointed his way.) Allen is currently establishing a university press at Columbia State College in Georgia. "I never thought I'd be running a university press, but here I am!" Having been involved in student editing since high school, Allen was a section editor for *Gulf Coast* and later its Editor-in-Chief, after finishing his PhD. He did his MFA at the Iowa Writers Workshop and has recently established an international literary prize, the Donald Jordan Prize for Literary Excellence. "I compartmentalize my writing practice and the administrative work of the press," he explained, "That's the only way to do it." Part of his day is for his own writing, always.

Allen described how the new press at Columbia State College has a number of undergraduate student interns. "They do everything here—read manuscripts, do the office work, even confer on publications." Allen has also taken students on international service trips to Guatemala, where the students teach English as a Second Language and help build cook stoves in villages that utilize plant-base fuels. For a while he ran the multicultural imprint 2040 at Santa Fe Writers Project, a New Mexico publisher which also runs a literary magazine.

And speaking of teaching English abroad, a number of student editors I have worked with over the years have spent time in other parts of the world after finishing their studies—teaching writing and editing in English. If you are interested in travel and teaching, consider doing a translation certificate while you are at university, or a certificate in teaching English as a foreign language. For more information on those opportunities, ask your academic advisor and check out https://www.tefl.org/en-us/.

Graduate School

It is not unusual for student editors to plan on graduate school in creative writing—in most cases a Masters of Fine Arts program (MFA). The best thing about graduate study is the opportunity to focus on your field—no more general education requirements (not entirely true, but mostly) while you begin to build a professional network and lifelong writing practice. Be warned, however, that an MFA in creative writing is less likely to be a doorway to an academic job than a PhD in creative writing will be. An MFA used to be a terminal degree in creative writing. These days it might lead to further work in the arts nonprofit sector or an academic appointment, but about forty years ago PhD programs in creative writing started cropping up, mostly with an eye toward training creative writers for academia. Today, many of the top PhD programs in creative writing require an MFA for entrance. However, many tenured faculty in creative writing programs simply have MFAs and a number of book publications. You have to publish. A lot of assistant professor jobs now require one or two books before you even think about compiling your application materials. You don't have to have a PhD to work in academia—ask the thousands of adjuncts (underpaid faculty who work on contract instead of appointment) who teach first year writing courses.

This is to say, again, that someone who is a self-starter and works hard at getting published can obviously do a lot better in the academic literary

world with an MFA than your average freelance writer. You have to love
teaching, however. There are a lot of writers, of all kinds, who do not live
and/or work in academia at all and who do not have MFAs or teach. Or
they teach—they make their living teaching—just not in higher ed or K-12.
You follow me? Many writers have made a living from community teaching.
Take a look at the many writing workshops available on the web, or perhaps
in your city/town/region. What fits your situation, your drive to engage in
writing and editing? Writers write. They work hard on their writing, no
matter what they do to pay the rent. An academic program in creative
writing can perhaps expedite your exposure to a lot of opportunities in the
national literary realm. The best part of graduate study may be that you get
a cohort, a collection of other writers you go through the writing program
with—writers who may become your go-to editors/readers for years to
come. Connections.

MFA programs are more or less structured according to poetry, fiction,
and nonfiction. Some have recently included subgenres like sci-fi and YA
(young adult), even literary editing and publishing. Some of the newest are
multi-genre. You can choose between a residential program (you have to be
there during the academic year—the non-pandemic years) and others are
"low-res" where you meet with your cohort, together with all the faculty,
once or twice a year for a week or two in groups. (You have to travel. Or
meet your groups online.) In either situation, there are workshops, readings,
and an opportunity to network. Most of the work in a low-res program is
done remotely, all year, online. (I suspect many residential programs will
permanently transform to a hybrid-type low-res in the coming years.) People
with established professions sometimes prefer low-res programs because
they can keep their day jobs. Ask yourself what fits you best—would you
rather stay where you are, with a job you might not want to leave, or are
you ready to make some big changes in your life?

Here are some basic questions you might ask yourself about embarking
on an MFA, accompanied by a few guiding notes:

- Where are you willing to live? Never apply to a residential program
  in a place you don't want to live. You will only have to be there
  for two or three years, but be honest with yourself about what you
  need. No snow? No unbearable heat? Be reasonable about who you
  are and what you need to thrive.

- What's the cost of living in the area? There are some wonderful
  programs in places like New York City and San Francisco, but if
  you have to live under a bridge in order to afford tuition it probably
  won't work out. You can find calculators for cost of living on the
  web, based on zip codes—check them out.

- Take a careful look at who teaches in these programs and familiarize
  yourself with their work. This is not to say that they will only teach
  you to write just like they do, but reading their work will at least

give you an idea of the program's aesthetic. Are the faculty diverse? If you are an experimental poet and the poetry faculty at University X all write in form, you might think twice about getting the support you need for what you want to do.

- What is the reputation of the program you are interested in? There is always Iowa, and all the lore surrounding the Iowa Writers Workshop. Ask around, look for further info on the programs you are considering, and talk to your creative writing professors. Ask the programs you are interested in if you can talk to a current student. Take everything with a grain of salt, however, *and* don't ignore the obvious.

- Don't be afraid to call a creative writing program's office and ask questions, but don't be asking about parks and restaurants—be very direct with actual questions about their curriculum (which you can find online in the university's catalogue) or extra-curricular opportunities, Teaching Assistantships, Scholarships, travel funds, office space for grad students, etc. You can ask if anyone is slated to be on leave or sabbatical (you don't want to show up only to find that the writer you wanted to work with is gone for two years). Listen carefully. If it's possible, arrange for a visit to the program during a regular semester—especially if they have offered you a spot but you aren't sure if it's a fit.

- Decisions on an incoming class are made by faculty and made first on the quality of the writing. Send your best work in your application, obviously. Just like with publishing, faculty at creative writing programs who are choosing a cohort for the coming year will have a very few students who everyone agrees are tops. Then there are a larger number of those who have to be discussed and decided on. If you end up in that batch, just know this: all your submitted materials count. No one is brought in on the basis of their GRE score (in fact many graduate programs don't use those anymore), but if everything else is equal and a recommendation letter is stellar or the sample critical writing is near perfect … let's just say that you might get a little bump.

- If you have been an editor of a literary journal and want to keep doing that work, find a place that has a good (or promising) literary journal. Find out more about that journal and how much opportunity you may have to work there. In some cases, if you include your interest in journal work with your application materials, they may actually send you an airplane ticket to get there sooner. On the other hand, if you do not want to do any more journal work, don't spend time highlighting your editorial experience as if you were interested in doing more of that work. No one likes bait and switch.

The stereotype of the writer, alone in an attic, half out of his mind (likely an annoying poet with a drug and alcohol problem) is about as far from the truth as any other stereotype. Just about any writer you have heard of works hard, keeps a schedule, and puts their writing time *first*. Writers will tell you a variety of things in interviews ("The only thing I know how to do is write," or "I sit down every day to work"), but the bottom line is that they do the work regularly—and that's not just the creative words-on-a-page work. Writers send their work to journals; they research agents and/or publishers. They figure out which periodicals and publishers are the best bet for their style of writing. They discuss the latest news and trends with other writers and editors. Most of them do a lot of things: judge a contest, do a visiting writer gig, show up for a panel or book signing, organize a reading series at the local library. These activities pay, but not much. As an undergraduate editor programming events you have gotten to know how much more there is to becoming a writer. This experience will serve you well if you decide to head down the path of the writing life.

For your literary academic program search, let us go back to AWP for a moment. On their website they also host their "Guide to Writing Programs" https://www.awpwriter.org/guide/guide_writing_programs which includes just about every academic writing program in the United States and a few beyond. This searchable database includes a short blurb on the program plus a link to the program websites. Do not forget to look at the official university catalogue for information on the curriculum of ANY program you are seriously considering. This takes a little time and patience, but you don't want to show up and be (un)pleasantly surprised that this particular MFA program has you taking required courses that don't make sense to you. (Caveat: those classes may make wonderful sense once you take them, so don't throw the baby out, etc.)

MFA programs grew exponentially for a while before the turn of the century, but not so much recently. In fact some have shut down. (Undergraduate creative writing programs have grown faster in recent years, and many of those do have associated graduate programs in creative writing and even graduate programs in composition and rhetoric.) Part of this pause in the growth of MFA programs has to do with a particular model of those programs, mostly true of low-res but not entirely. It takes advantage of an economic trend in higher ed toward making money. Graduate tuition is not cheap, and faculty at most low-res programs are paid on contract, not as appointment. (Academic appointment can matter because the faculty person is fully committed to the institution, has a salary and benefits. This by no means guarantees that you will get better leadership and mentoring from a tenured/tenure-track versus contract faculty member. Pretty much like every other personal relationship, good mentoring depends upon building a connection.) No institution of higher learning really has enough money because the traditional model depends on public support of education, and that has been under fire lately. (Plenty of private universities have impressive endowments—and many don't.) People who think they can write and have the money to buy tuition can learn some tricks of the trade and start their professional writing with an MFA. People who do not have the money for tuition can find scholarships (they exist) but should proceed only because they love—absolutely adore—the writing life. Proceed to an MFA with your eyes open.

Student Editing as Part of the Undergraduate Curriculum

This penultimate section of this book is addressed to the faculty advisor, regular faculty, and administrators who support undergraduate literary magazines. Magazine work, editing, nonprofit organizations, websites, writing, literary citizenship—these are all areas of professional work that you support. Undergraduate courses on literature—from Shakespeare's sonnets to Twitter novels—teach students how to parse the written word. Rhetoric and composition courses dive deep into our history as thinkers and writers and readers. Literary theory helps readers, researchers, and writers understand what is going on in the current era and how people in other eras conceived of their texts and times. Translation and multilingual texts connect us across boundaries that we (thankfully) see disappearing before our eyes as we more fully understand that the world belongs to all of us equally. As the world therefore gets "traveled" and our connections show how dependent we are on each other, helping students to use new skills in real time is not just an extra gift, it is a necessity. There is no time to waste.

If you are interested in undergraduate curriculum, look at some of the schools that are ranked highly in English and languages on US News and World Report's website for university rankings. Check out the curriculum for undergraduates at the top 100 and note that many offering creative writing degrees include editing courses, editing internships, journal practicum courses, composition history, and library research classes as required study. Giving all your majors the opportunity to earn course credit by working at a student-run journal (advised, of course, by attentive faculty) can help them see an immediate future beyond your campus. And while you may think that editors, like writers, are born let me assure you that talented students are those given opportunity and training (in your lit and rhetoric and media courses, too). The paths students may take after their experience with literary production include a broad number of activities, including the many mentioned here, plus the usual law school (copyright and international trade, for instance) and further academic study in a variety of other fields. If your students know how to manage a magazine, work with texts and people, they can probably manage their careers.

If you do not have the patience to look up all that information from dozens of university catalogues, then consider this: we are in the information age. You are experts in some form of research on texts that were produced by writers who are largely dead and gone—or writing as profusely as you read every day. All of those texts had publishers (and editors and etc.). It seems only natural that our language departments would support not only the final product of textual production, but the process a text goes through to get there as well. Rhetoric and composition has known this for a long time. It might be obvious that helping your students engage the process of their own writing might be well supported by highlighting the process of publishing. Why not use your undergraduate magazine as the central focus, or shared focus, of your degree programs? While many faculty advisors will tell you that the work they do is often seen as something extra that faculty must do—sometimes ascribed to someone that the other faculty are relieved to know is taking care of it—consider raising that profile. Get more faculty involved. Many advisors I know will tell you that working side by side with undergraduates (and/or graduate students) is the most fun they've had. It hardly seems like teaching. I suggest giving them offloads—the work they do with a fresh group of students each semester is, after all, teaching.

In a recent conversation with poet and Professor Wayne Miller from University of Colorado Denver (he is the Editor-in-Chief of *Copper Nickel*—you've already been introduced), he expressed grand appreciation for being able to bring in undergraduates to help at the press. *Copper Nickel* is a professional literary journal and the upper editors are all faculty at University of Colorado Denver—and accomplished writers themselves. "Every Monday and Thursday morning at 9:30 I meet with undergraduates, 8–15 students, and we read the slush pile together. We operate like an advanced undergraduate lab." Wayne and the students read, talk, and compare impressions on the manuscripts they are processing—they have a broad range of impromptu discussion on the work of *Copper Nickel* and publishing in general. He also teaches a publishing practicum class every other semester. "It functions as an inductive lens to literary publishing." Admittedly, he says, more time with the students means more of his time. (They do not have a graduate program in creative writing at his campus, no teaching assistants or graduate advisors.) He is compensated for his time at *Copper Nickel* through his academic contract. It's part of his course load, his teaching time—but the time spent with students doing publication work expands exponentially his time commitment to the press. "They start as assistant editors, but move on to associate editors—we even have senior editors, post-bac students who are still in the area and have worked for *Copper Nickel* for years." The magazine offers internships as well. Interns compile author bios, work with proofs, and engage in all kinds of necessary press work alongside Wayne and the other faculty editors.

As mentioned in the Introduction to this book, undergraduate literary magazines are potentially entering an era of primacy. Again and again I see new curriculum that puts undergraduate student magazines (or professional university literary magazines) at the center of the undergrad (and sometimes graduate) curriculum—because they teach skills that students will need when they leave the university. The old-fashioned jokes about English majors as baristas have gone cold—aside from the fact that so many coffee places have closed during the pandemic. And because of the pandemic and the recent push from Black Lives Matter moving forward our national discussion on persistent racism in American, much work has been done at universities to shift the focus, the course work and the activities, to broader offerings— finally including more voices and addressing the awareness that time had been wasted by *not* looking at the texts and processes typically considered marginalized. Universities seem poised to make that inclusive switch. Some would say publishing is right there behind them—or will be soon enough when the big publishers realize the expanse of reading publics they are not yet serving. There's more international awareness, too, at universities—and awareness of the social changes connected to our varied cultures' online presence. How could we not take advantage of this moment to rethink our undergrad curriculum and put real-life, hands-on learning front and center? How can we *not* bring brilliant students into a situation where they can try out their skills and interests and discover their genius?

A Final Word for Students

Experience as an editor at an undergraduate literary magazine will pay you back again and again. Easy for me to say. The statement is not intended to push you to kill yourself over a thankless volunteer gig. Rather, I want to encourage all undergrad creative writers (and literature and rhet comp and other students inside/outside the humanities who love to read and/or write) to engage in an activity that gives you a taste of leadership and camaraderie in the workplace. Running an undergraduate literary magazine gives you a chance to apply what you've learned in many other classes, to grapple with ways to turn theories into practice, to make mistakes and learn from them, to find out what it is you love about your work and take that forward to your future.

For the Graduate Student Advisors reading this book, lucky you—helping undergraduates put together a literary magazine is humbling and exciting. If you already know you are a teacher, being a literary magazine advisor is the place for you. It is the best teaching experience for hands-on learning, as chaotic as it can be. Be prepared to tear your hair out on occasion, and always keep your eye on the best outcome: giving students a chance to try out their skills on a project that has their name on it. It's true that not a lot of institutions heap praise on the head of someone who oversees this enterprise—or not yet. But believe me there is a whole department of people who are grateful to you for taking up this project of helping to run an undergraduate literary magazine. You too are supporting what they do in their reading courses every day.

If you are reading this book because you are considering starting your own magazine, then I hope the general outline here is helpful. If you are a former student editor, you already know the work. (If you have more ideas on a second edition to this book, send me your thoughts.) Literary journals come and go, but that is no reason to *not* create your own journal and give your publishing vision a firm foundation.

As I'm working on this book, we are (a lot us, some of us more than others) inside alone, looking out at a world changed, ready to get back to spending more time together. The pandemic situation and the hopeful promise of working against systemic, institutional racism bring to mind our careful judgment. What can we do with the situation in front of us? How can we best formulate the inevitable changes? Surely we can create something new that works for writers inside and outside academia. For the future of publishing and the reading public, there will always be new material to consider. Right now we must handle what we have and take some risks on content and delivery, intentionally making some changes we know are necessary—imagining forward. Those of you who have an affinity for editing and a dream of publishing will no doubt develop the words and put out the message that we can find a better way.

APPENDIX A

Websites Listing Print and Online Journals

CLMP (Community of Literary Magazines and Publishers) (https://www.clmp.org/) is another nonprofit that's been around for a while and plays a supporting role for literary publishers: *"We—the Community of Literary Magazines and Presses (formerly the Council of Literary Magazines and Presses)—are hundreds of small publishers creating print and digital books, magazines, online publications, chapbooks and zines, who have come together to do our work as publishers better and to organize around a shared set of beliefs."* They, too, maintain a searchable list of independent literary publishers with direct links to websites and a searchable listing of "Calls for Submission" where you can buy advertising space for contests, awards, or simply submissions. While a membership in the organization can be helpful to a student journal, and isn't terribly expensive ($125), there is plenty to see on the website that's free. If you do buy a membership, use it. The resources available would be effective classroom material for a publication practicum course as well.

Duotrope (https://duotrope.com/) is a slightly different wonderland of writer—and artist—resources. It's a subscription service designed to help writers and artists place their work with journals, agents, and publishers. *"Duotrope is an established, award-winning resource for writers and artists. We help you save time finding publishers or agents for your work, so you can focus on creating. Our market listings are up to date and full of information you won't find elsewhere. We also offer submission trackers, custom searches, deadline calendars, statistical reports, and extensive interviews."* This organization is a business but does not allow ads (they are seriously a subscription service)—and they have recently offered a submission manager function. They are very strict about their "eligibility criteria."

New Pages The ultimate listing of literary magazines (https://www.newpages.com/) gives the viewer very quick description of thousands of journals. *"Newpages.com is news, information, and guides to literary magazines, independent publishers, creative writing programs, alternative periodicals, indie bookstores, writing contests, and more."* This website includes easy search functions and links to publications they list. They also include an incredibly helpful subsection on undergraduate journals: https://www.

newpages.com/magazines/undergrad-lit-mags where entries are organized by state—on average about ten per state or roughly 500 undergraduate journals.

Poets and Writers began as a print magazine publishing articles on the art and business of creative writing and has perfected the art of disseminating information to writers. *"Founded in 1970, Poets & Writers is the nation's largest nonprofit organization serving creative writers. Our mission? To foster the professional development of poets and writers, to promote communication throughout the literary community, and to help create an environment in which literature can be appreciated by the widest possible public."* Their website, *"pw.org, includes the **Directory of Poets & Writers**, which provides contact information, publication credits, and biographical information for more than 9,300 authors; databases of **literary magazines and journals, small and independent presses, literary agents, MFA programs, writing contests,** and **literary places;** a national literary events calendar; and select content from* **Poets & Writers Magazine.**" Student journals can also buy advertising space in the magazine for reduced prices.

Websites Helpful for Undergraduate Literary Magazine Organizations

(See CLMP above for their support functions—on the pull-down menu under "Join," see "Benefits.")

AWP If your university or college is a member program at Association of Writers and Writing Programs (AWP—mentioned several times in this book) you may have access to a number of resources through that membership. Check with your program director. *"AWP provides support, advocacy, resources, and community to nearly 50,000 writers, 550 college and university creative writing programs, and 150 writers' conferences and centers. Our mission is to foster literary achievement, advance the art of writing as essential to a good education, and serve the makers, teachers, students, and readers of contemporary writing."*

Editing For a bit of background on anything from grammar to contracts, the wild index at Writers and Editors (http://www.writersandeditors.com/) is a fount of quick (if not always strictly accurate) information. This website is the work of one Pat McNees, self-described writer and editor. For a quick list of easy editing marks try this quick list from the Chicago Manual of Style website: https://www.chicagomanualofstyle.org/help-tools/proofreading-marks.html. And for a useful listing of editing and publishing terms, try https://www.editorialdepartment.com/publishing-glossary/ or https://www.tcbok.org/wiki/research/glossary/glossary-writingediting-terms/ which is a website for tech writers and has way more information than you will need.

For simple publishing terminology, try https://booklogix.com/publishing-terminology/.

Grammar and Punctuation There are a ton of websites on grammar and usage, but Daily Grammar is both staid and *fun* for the grammar nerds in your organization: https://dailygrammarlessons.blogspot.com/. And while Grammarly software can make you want to throw your computer out a window, there are plenty of websites that can help you unknot a number of questions your staff may have about punctuation and grammar during proofreading: try https://dictionary.cambridge.org/us/grammar/british-grammar/pronouns_1 for simple rules or consider a downloadable cheat-sheet for your editors https://www.apu.edu/live_data/files/288/basic_punctuation_rules.pdf

Information on Literary Magazines *The Review Review* is an online magazine *about* literary magazines. "The Review Review *is an open-access journal supporting writers, editors, students, and teachers by offering reviews of recent issues of literary magazines, interviews with editors of literary magazines, and features on the publishing industry.*" This website would be helpful for a literary magazine publication course—it's one layer deeper than the other listings here. These articles are written by a wide range of contributors on a plethora of topics—they invite you to become a reviewer at the click of a button on their home page.

Building a Website

Domain Names and Hosting should be purchased through reputable companies with decent customer service (though hopefully none is needed—keep careful track of all your login info). You might try GoDaddy (https://www.godaddy.com/) or Just Host (https://www.justhost.com/) or Bluehost (https://www.bluehost.com/).

Ecommerce If you are going to engage in any ecommerce (sell magazines, t-shirts, conference registrations, or other merchandise from your website or phones) you will need a "store." The most obvious choice is Square (https://squareup.com/us/en/online-store) but there are others, such as WooCommerce (https://woocommerce.com/) and Shopify (https://www.shopify.com/) which all function with WordPress. Before you open an online store, have a deep and meaningful discussion with your local web guru about security for your website and the relative costs of engaging one of these services.

Website Builder The obvious answer is WordPress (https://wordpress.com/). But this is only the beginning. There is also Squarespace (https://www.squarespace.com/) and Wix (https://www.wix.com/) and the thousands of themes each of these to choose from.

APPENDIX B

Sample Acceptance Letter

Hello [SubmitterFirstName],

Thank you for sending your work. We would like to publish your piece "[Title]" in the next volume of [your magazine's name]. Please reply to this email to let us know if "[Title]" is still available. We ask for First North American Serial Rights (meaning we retain the rights until publication, then they revert back to you). We also need written confirmation that you are accepting our offer of publication in Volume (x), Spring 20XX.

We will also need a brief bio (50–100 words) if you didn't include one with your cover letter or if you wish to update the one we already have. Please include your physical mailing address and preferred email address.

We are looking forward to publishing your work. Once we receive your reply to this email, the section editor will contact you about any final edits.

Kind regards,
The Editors
[your magazine's name]

Sample Rejection Letter

Dear [Author Name],

Thank you for your patience as we reviewed your submission "[Title]." After careful consideration, we regret that it does not meet the current needs of [your magazine's name]. We admire your dedication to your craft and appreciate your interest in our publication.

Warmly,
The Editors
[your magazine's name]

Sample Publication Agreement

As long as you get a writer's or artist's written permission (in an email, for example) to publish their work, you won't need to go so far as an actual "publishing agreement." The link below, however, is an example of a template that publishers might use for longer works: https://www.priorilegal.com/legal-forms-and-documents/publishing-agreement

Sample Style Sheet

You will have to decide a few very simple things, like when to use m dashes or n dashes, how to handle numbers, and correct hyphenation—plus so much more. Many magazines start with the basics from the Chicago Manual of Style and then create their own specifics for an easy-reference one- or two-page guide for editors and proofreaders. Here is an example of a simple style sheet (your group can create your own after one session of editing, believe me): https://libroediting.com/2016/02/04/using-a-style-sheet-for-editors-and-proofreaders/

Sample Schedule

A more complete schedule should be built using a web calendar. If you maintain a Google Drive site for your documents, you can use the Google Calendar function so the entire staff can view or edit. The basic idea of a list such as the one below is that you can see, on one page, all your major dates and deadlines—and quickly review those during a meeting with the staff.

Undergrad Lit Mag Schedule 20xx—20xx

Meeting with Editor-in-Chief, co-managing editors, web editor, faculty advisor, and graduate advisor

FALL

August 25th (2:30-7 p.m.)—Fall RSO Festival (Rec Center)
August 30th—interview with University Development team—noon
September 1st—Ranghal Prize winners announced
September 6th (7:30 p.m.)—meeting with Board of Advisors
September 15th—Prize submissions due
September 20th (7 p.m.)—All Staff Meeting

September 27th (7 p.m.) READING—Tanget's, with open mic
MONTH OF OCTOBER—FUNDAISING CAMPAIGN
October 3rd—submission deadline for issue #17 (can be moved to the 7th
or 8th)
October 20th—all choices made from slush (start with permissions, editing,
and bios)
October 26th—Hallow-reading (place to be determined)
November—START ADVERTIZING FOR POETRY AND PROSE AWARD
November 3rd—evening sequencing meeting (all editing done, all manuscripts
due to Editor-in-Chief by noon
November 5th—Saturday, all day, Fundraiser at Library room 143
November 10th—Proofing packets go to all editors
November 13th—Proofing meeting, Library (afternoon)
November 17th—Issue #17 goes to printer and web editor
December 6th—Launch Party—Hazlit Cafe (7 p.m.)

SPRING

January 9th—deadline for Poetry and Prose Award submissions
January 10th—submissions go to graduate students
January 18th—Poetry and prose submissions go to final readers (profs)
January 31st—Reading and Poetry and Prose winners due
February 1st—Poetry and Prose winners announced
February 2nd—All Staff Meeting
February 8th to 12th—staff attends AWP and Bookfair
February 11th Submissions for Issue #18 due
February 14th—Busking for Valentine's Day—Student Center
February 14th—all choices made from slush for #18
February 28th—Reading at Barker and Tone
March 10th—Sequencing Meeting
March 12th-19th—SPRING BREAK
March 21st—Proofing Packets
March 25th—afternoon proofing meeting
March 28th—Issue #18 to printer and web editor
April 1st—applications for faculty adviser (timeline TBA)
April 19th—Issue #18 Launch party—Poetry and Prose at the library
May 14th—Interviews begin for next year's staff
May 31st—Announcement of new staff
June 1st—Ranghal Prize opens for submissions
August 1st—Ranghal Prize submissions close and go to judges

Books About Editing

What Editors Do—ed. Peter Gina
The Subversive Copy Editor: Advice From Chicago—Carol Saller

The Copy Editor's Handbook and Workbook—Amy Einsohn, Marilyn Schwartz, Erika Buky
Developmental Editing: A Handbook for Freelancers, Authors, and Publishers—Scott Norton
The Editor's Companion—Steve Dunham
The Chicago Manual of Style

Noteworthy Printers (not mentioned in the chapters)

Publisher's Group West https://www.pgw.com/
Book Mobile https://www.bookmobile.com/book-production/print-literary-journals-magazines/
PrintNinja https://printninja.com/printing-resource-center/printing-options/book-services
Dazzle Printing https://www.dazzleprinting.com/online-printing/magazine-printing/

Sample Staff Application

Applicant Information

Please note: our magazine accepts staff applications from undergraduates at the University of XXXXX and its affiliated colleges.

First Name:	Last Name:
Position Desired:	Major/Minor:
# Hours Available/Week	What year are you in your degree program?
Email Address:	Expected Graduation Date:
Cell Phone:	Permanent Street Address:
Alternate Phone:	City, State, Zip Code:

1. Why are you interested in this position?
2. List any previous experience you have with publishing/journals. (Attach Resumé/CV if available)
3. What do you believe to be the [your journal's name here] aesthetic?

Please return this completed application to the XXXXX mailbox located in the UX English Department copy room, or email to xxxxxxeditors@gmail.com

INDEX